PANHANDLE COWBOY

PANHANDLE COWBOY

John R. Erickson

Foreword by
Larry McMurtry

Photographs by
Bill Ellzey

UNIVERSITY OF NEBRASKA PRESS
Lincoln and London

Chapter 2, "Ranching in Beaver County," was first published, in somewhat different form, in the Spring 1978 issue of *Oklahoma Today*, pp. 26–30.

Library of Congress Cataloging in Publication Data

Erickson, John R 1943–
  Panhandle cowboy.

  1. Erickson, John R., 1943– 2. Crown Ranch, Okla.
3. Ranch life—Oklahoma—Beaver Co. 4. Beaver Co.,
Okla.—Social life and customs. 5. Cowboys—Okla-
homa—Beaver Co.—Biography. 6. Beaver Co., Okla.
—Biography. I. Ellzey, Bill. II. Title.
F702.B4F733   976.6'14'050924 [B]   79–24929
ISBN 0–8032–1803–6

To my father,
Joseph W. Erickson

CONTENTS

ILLUSTRATIONS

FOREWORD

Crafts, traditions, and ways of life are vulnerable to impersonal forces—cosmic, geopolitical, or economic—that take no account of their value or their appeal. This book is about one such threatened craft: namely, cowboying.

As a craft cowboying has only existed for about 120 years, has been in decline for at least half that time, and has never involved very many people; yet its potency in American myth is practically unrivaled. Part of this potency can be explained by the fact that it is a pastoral craft—in the increasingly suburbanized American environment even to think about the pastoral brings a kind of uplift. But if there can be said to be a core element in cowboying, that element is probably independence. In point of fact, as John Erickson repeatedly makes clear, cowboys depend on a good many things besides themselves—on horses, neighbors, and luck, to name only three—but even so, and despite the fact that they are ultimately somebody's employee, the practice of their craft allows them a far greater sense of independence than most Americans now feel. It is in the join-

ing of a deep and rhythmic pastoralism with a challenging
and sustaining independence that the resonance of the
cowboy myth resides.

Panhandle Cowboy is a sensitive, admirably straightfor-
ward book about the texture of modern cowboying in the
Oklahoma Panhandle. These truthful and affectionate de-
scriptions of life and work in that severe locale serve to rein-
force an old point: that hardship and risk are woven deeply
into the appeal of cowboying. Often as not the elements
themselves provide all the hardship that anyone could well
want. Should the weather happen to be comfortable, animals or the cattle market will contribute the hardship. In
this one regard cowboys resemble desert Arabs: their best
qualities are forged by extreme conditions. Enrich or
suburbanize a Bedouin or a cowboy and taste, vigor, and
sense of craft are soon lost. Keep them out where the winds
blow, the sands storm, and the animals resist all reasonable effort and they remain superb workmen, alert, hu-
morous, and subtle.

If one compares this book with the few classics of cowboying—Andy Adams's *The Log of a Cowboy*, or Teddy
Blue Abbott's *We Pointed Them North*—one can fairly judge
what has endured and what has been lost. Most obviously,
what has been lost is the open range and the expanding
market; what has remained is weather, horses, and the
comradeship of roundup crews. And, of course, cattle, but
as John Erickson points out in an accurate passage, cowboys do not love cattle. Cattle provide the basis of the craft,
but I have no doubt that many a cowboy has wished for
more responsive creatures upon which to expend his skill
and effort. As Mr. Erickson says, cattle are simply there,
like the wind and the landscape, a part of the rhythm, a
part of the life.

LARRY MCMURTRY

ACKNOWLEDGMENTS

I want to thank the following people who helped me along the way: Keith Good, Dr. Robert H. Mayo, Jim and Marilyn Gregg, Professor Paul F. Boller, Professor Donald Worcester, Mary Dykema, and Marc Simmons.

And I want to thank Kris, who has put up with me through twelve years of marriage. She has developed a very nice way of kicking me out of bed at 4:30 A.M. and sending me off to my typewriter.

PANHANDLE COWBOY

1
THE CROWN RANCH

Most hired hands and cowboys on America's ranches make their homes in unlovely shacks, cow camps, or trailer houses. From January of 1974 until May of 1978 I worked as a cowboy in the sandhills of Beaver County, Oklahoma. My family and I made our home in a Greek mansion, surrounded by statues of Venus and Sappho and bas relief plaques bearing the images of Roman gods.

After a day on horseback, I bathed in a tub made of black marble and drew my bath water from a spigot made in the image of a swan. The water spewed from its mouth. I read my *Livestock Weekly* and *Cattleman* magazine in the light of five glittering chandeliers, any one of which I could not have borrowed enough money to buy. At the age of three, my son Scottie began playing bulldozer and cattle truck in an atrium that occupied the center of the house. It was open at the top and separated from the rest of the house by glass walls on three sides. Presiding over the atrium was a solemn life-sized statue of a woman holding an urn.

3

The owner of the ranch had inherited five thousand acres of grassland from his grandmother. He chose as his brand a four-sided figure which he called a crown. He was a man whose interests were not satisfied by the routine chores of animal husbandry, and who found life on the ranch confining, dull, and lacking in cultural opportunities. To amuse and express himself, he decided to build a show place on the prairie. He spent five years haggling with architects, fretting over blueprints, begging contractors to finish the job, and doing much of the construction work himself, and by the time the Greek mansion was completed in 1974, he was so weary of it all that he put the ranch in trust and left the country. He had never slept a single night in the Prairie Parthenon he had spent five years building.

He put the ranch in the hands of Keith Good, the trust officer of the First Bank and Trust Company of Booker, Texas. Keith's first job was to find a man to manage the property. He and I had grown up together in the small town of Perryton, Texas, and had known each other all our lives. Keith knew that I had ranching experience and that I was looking around for a ranch job. In the fall of 1973, he told me about the Crown Ranch and asked if I would be interested in managing it for him. We drove up into the Oklahoma Panhandle, sixty miles northeast of Perryton, and looked it over.

The ranch was located in the sandhills, fifteen miles northeast of Beaver, the county seat of Beaver County, Oklahoma. These sagebrush-covered hills are part of a large formation that begins some twenty miles west of Beaver and run all the way to Woodward, Oklahoma. For a hundred miles along the course of the Beaver River, the sandhills begin at the flood plain on the north bank and extend four to seven miles to the north, rising two or three hundred feet above the level of the river. There the sandhills merge with the tighter soils and buffalo-grama grass country of the Cimarron River watershed.

The Prairie Parthenon.

   The Beaver River is the only major watercourse in the Oklahoma Panhandle. It heads in New Mexico around Capulin Mountain, enters the Panhandle southwest of Boise City, takes a little jog down into Sherman County, Texas, flows past Guymon and Beaver and Laverne, and joins Wolf Creek near Fort Supply. On some maps it is called the North Canadian, but to the people of the Panhandle, it is the Beaver River until it joins Wolf Creek, and then it assumes the grander title of North Canadian.

   The Crown Ranch did not adjoin the river. It was located in the high and dry country, with the south fence a mile and a half north of the river. There was no live water on the ranch, not one spring or creek, although it was sufficiently watered by ten windmills. There were, by my count, five trees on the entire five thousand acres. It sat on top of one of the largest natural gas fields in Oklahoma, and there were five producing gas wells on the ranch.

   After looking over the ranch, I told Keith I wanted the job, and we agreed that I would assume my duties in January. I would be the only employee on the ranch, which meant that I could call myself either the hired man or the manager. I functioned in both capacities. I did most of the work myself, and Keith gave me the authority to make all the decisions on the everyday operation of the ranch. He trusted me and respected my judgment, and he let me run the ranch just as though it were my own. I couldn't have asked for a better man to work under. But it wasn't my ranch, and I always tried to remember that. Whenever I faced a major decision, such as the marketing of cattle or the purchase of winter feed, I did not make a move without consulting him first. Usually he went along with my suggestions, but there were times when he came up with a better idea. The arrangement worked very well for both of us, and the only contract we ever had was a handshake.

   On January 7, 1974, Keith and I drove from one end of the ranch to the other. He showed me the pastures, the feed grounds, the windmills, and all the roads and trails that wound through the ranch. When he left that afternoon, I was on my own. I knew very little about the cattle, though Keith had warned me that they were an unruly bunch. There were four horses on the place, and neither Keith nor I knew anything about them either. In the tiny sixteen-by-twenty-foot barn I found bagged feed, salt, tools, medicine, saddles, blankets, bridles, spurs, and bits in no particular order. I knew just enough about the ranch so that I could drive around without getting lost. And that is where I began.

I spent much of my first three months riding horseback in the afternoon, studying the pastures and the lay of the land. I found that almost half the acreage of the ranch was under one fence in the west pasture, four square miles of country that ranged from buffalo flats on the north to brushy sandhills on the south. The 1,300-acre middle pasture was the roughest on the ranch, with ravines on the west and high sandhills on the east. There were two smaller pastures on the east end of the ranch, the big east with 640 acres and the little east with 240 acres.

Most of this country, I soon discovered, was inaccessible by two-wheel-drive pickup. In the sandy soils you risked getting stuck, while in the tighter soils you found your way blocked by draws and washouts. It was also difficult to see the cattle in this terrain. A good-sized herd could lose itself in one of the sink holes in the sandy country, and unless you rode right up to them on horseback, you would never know they were there.

A-horseback, I got my first look at the cattle. I had been told that they were as wild as deer, and they were. I had grown up working on ranches down in Texas and had been taught that there was no better way of checking cattle than to ride through them on horseback. On this ranch, that was not possible. When they saw a horse—it didn't matter whether he was moving at a high lope or at a walk, toward them or away from them—when these cattle saw a horse in the pasture, they turned and ran.

To a cowboy who enjoyed riding quietly through a bunch of cows, checking udders and eyes and admiring the new crop of calves, that proved a terrible frustration. Often they would spot me when I was still a quarter mile away. At that distance I could see their white faces, all turned toward me. Then one cow would bawl for her calf. Two or three more would begin to bawl and mill. Then one would break into a run. The others would fall into a line, and off they would go to the back side of the pasture. Another bunch of cattle in another part of the pasture would see them running and they would start running, too—even though they had not actually seen the horse and might be a mile or more away. Within minutes the whole pasture would be in an uproar, with cattle running everywhere. During those first months I learned a management principle that was always good on the Crown Ranch: any cow that didn't run from my horse was sick.

In 1974 we were running Charolais bulls on Hereford cows. This crossing was used because the Charolais breeding produced a larger, heavier calf than straight Hereford breeding. It also caused calving problems because some of the Hereford cows did not have the bone structure or frame to deliver the big crossbred calves. I never had any trouble finding them. I appeared on horseback, the healthy cows vanished, and there would be one cow left, with a big crossbred calf halfway out of her body. Then all I had to do was drive her to the house while she sulled and attacked my horse.

If wild cattle made my job difficult, so did the weather. Weather is something cowboys live with every day, and that is why they rank among the world's most ardent followers of weather reports, even though forecasters are as often wrong as they are right. This is especially true in the plains country of the Texas and Oklahoma panhandles, where the weather is capricious and often violent. The weather outside intrudes on the cowboy's life and mood and can make a simple job difficult or impossible.

It didn't take me long to discover which element of nature would cause me the most misery in my new job. It was the wind. As a general proposition, the Oklahoma Panhandle is a windy place. In the winter, we were thrashed by north winds which produced a brutal form of cold that was reflected in the chill factor. It was not uncommon for the chill factor to reach thirty or forty degrees below zero in January. In March, a day of northerly gales was often followed by a day of southerly gales like slaps delivered to both sides of the face. And in the summertime our poor gardens and shrubs were roasted by blast-furnace winds out of the southwest.

The Panhandle is windy in general, and the ranch I managed was surely the windiest spot in the entire Panhandle. The owner had chosen to build his house, working pens, and barn on a bald hill. He did not care for trees, so he planted none. There was no protection whatever from the wrath of nature. This created a wonderful variety of problems for me. I discovered, for example, that in a high wind, gates and pickup doors could become lethal weapons. I once attempted to get out of the pickup in a high wind and almost got my head cut off. Another time I tried to close a heavy wooden gate against a strong south wind created by an approaching thunderstorm. I was blown backward, the gate flew open and smashed into the fence, and I said to hell with it and hunted a hole.

Another time, when I had been on the ranch about three months, I was feeding cattle one miserable windy, dusty day in March. I had parked my pickup on a feed ground located on a ridge, had managed to climb out the door without losing my head, and was waiting for the cattle to come in for their cottonseed cake. They looked as miserable as I felt. Their eyes were watering and rimmed with dust, their heads hung low, and their winter hair stood straight out from their sides, giving them a ragged appearance. I was leaning against the pickup, minding my own business, when a cow standing sixty feet upwind lifted her tail and began to relieve herself. Before I knew what was happening, my face and glasses were splattered with urine.

Roping in such wind was another source of torment. Most cowboys carry a rope on the saddle at all times and take some pride in their ability to use it. You practice this skill around the barn by roping cinder blocks, dummies, garbage cans, sawhorses, or passing dogs. Riding pastures, you take aim at fence posts and sagebrush. My practice periods were always conducted on still days, simply because on windy days I was never in the mood for roping. When the occasion arose for me to rope a calf in the pasture on a blustery day, when I rode a horse at thirty miles an hour into a thirty-mile-an-hour wind, when I pursued an elusive target that I might have had trouble noosing under ideal conditions, all my practice and timing amounted to nothing.

A set of working pens exposed to constant wind can be a torture chamber. A cowboy spends a lot of time around the corral. All cattle with special problems come to the pens: sick animals, cattle that must be shifted from one pasture to another, pregnant heifers, and cows with big udders that must be milked out. You feed horses in the pens, keep up your saddle horses for the night, and wean, train, and break colts in the pens. In the spring you brand calves there, and in the fall you ship cattle from the pens. The constant traffic of cattle and horses creates three by-products: hay, dust, and manure. In a high wind these dried elements are all swirling in the air. This means that if you find yourself in the corral on a windy day, your eyes will soon be filled with hay, dust, and powdered manure. If you open your mouth, your teeth will become brown and gritty. If you are performing veterinary chores where sterile conditions are desirable, you will not be pleased when you see flakes of manure floating around in the Lysol and water, or when the wind blows the bucket off a fence post and deposits your instruments in the dirt.

If you are working with horses, you will find that a high wind can transform a gentle horse into one that is skittish, and a skittish horse into one that is dangerous. Strange sounds and objects appear out of nowhere. An oil can that has lain in the weeds for months will suddenly come rolling into view. A bread wrapper blows out of the garbage can, flies through the air, and hits the horse on the nose. A feed sack sprouts wings, soars into the sky, and swoops down like an attacking bird. A gate comes unhooked and flies open.

When I first arrived on the ranch, I had never made any association between wind velocity and the behavior of horses. I learned quickly. I did not have to be run over and stepped on very many times before I began to understand that, on this particular ranch, there were certain days when you didn't want to be in the company of horses, especially broncs and colts. I was fortunate to have absorbed this lesson outside of a hospital, although I had some close calls— which only goes to prove that heaven often intervenes to protect a fool.

2
RANCHING IN BEAVER COUNTY

Ranching in the Oklahoma Panhandle is a risky and unpredictable venture. In the first place, the raw material in ranching is grass. Cattle eat the grass, and with their marvelous four-chambered stomach are able to convert coarse roughage (on which a human would quickly starve to death) into delicious beef (upon which humans are fond of dining). But grass does not grow without proper moisture, and even the shrewdest ranch managers have yet to produce a single raindrop.

The rancher is completely at the mercy of Mother Nature, and in the Panhandle she has often been accused of child abuse. The droughts of the thirties and fifties are deeply etched into the memories of cattlemen who survived them. And so are the legendary blizzards, such as the storm of 1886, which taught English and Scottish investors a bitter lesson about converting their cash into a product as perishable as cattle. And there are dust storms, hail storms, electrical storms, and, when you least expect and need them, floods.

A second factor that makes ranching unpredictable is the finished product: cattle. The primary disadvantage of cattle is that they are alive. Where an inanimate commodity such as steel can be crated, stored, and shipped with relative ease, cattle cannot. They are in the habit of eating and drinking every day, and when denied feed and water, they will respond by losing weight and quality—and therefore money. With live animals, even the simplest and most basic of business functions, inventory, becomes a chore. Before cattle can be counted, they must first be assembled. Before they are gathered from, say, a pasture of five square miles, they may jump a fence into the neighbor's pasture, hide in some brush along the river, or simply be overlooked in the sandhills. And even when they are gathered and the counting begins, three cowboys may come up with three different numbers. Counting cattle is not exactly like counting toothpicks on the kitchen table. It is more like counting a swarm of mosquitoes on the front porch.

Still, there is a predictable and orderly side to ranching, a routine of work that roughly follows the seasons. In the Panhandle, the first freeze can be expected around October 15. With a hard freeze, the grass ceases to grow and goes to sleep for the winter. It also begins to lose its food value, and the amount of protein it will yield to a range cow steadily declines until green grass comes again in the spring. This decline in nutritional value coincides with the arrival of cold weather, when a cow requires a certain level of protein and energy just to keep herself warm and to maintain her body weight through the winter. As a result, ranchers in this part of the country must begin feeding their cattle a protein supplement sometime between Thanksgiving and December 15, depending on range conditions.

The daily feed run is the most important ranch job in the winter. With sacks of feed in the back of his pickup, the rancher or his hired hand drives from one pasture to another, calling up the cattle. Some honk the pickup horn.

Crown Ranch cattle coming to feed on a snowy morning.

Others use a bull horn, an actual horn that is blown like a trumpet. Yet another will cup a hand around his mouth and bellow in his own distinctive manner, making a sound like "Wooooooo!" or "Hee-yo!" The object is to inform the cattle that dinner is served.

The feeding continues until green grass appears in the spring, usually between the middle of March and the middle of April. By then, flights of cranes, ducks, and geese have passed overhead, the wild plum has burst into bloom, and the days have become warm and balmy. More calves are being born every day, and the rancher begins preparing for the next major job, the spring roundup and branding.

Anyone who enjoys working around cattle cannot help feeling a bit of excitement with the approach of the spring roundup season. On a roundup morning, you get up at five o'clock, feed your horse some oats, saddle him in the moonlight, load him into the trailer, and arrive at a neighbor's ranch around six-thirty, when the sun is still a pink bud in the eastern sky. There you drink coffee and swap yarns with the other cowboys until the rest of the crew pulls in. The crew may be as small as five or as large as fifteen, depending on the size of the ranch and the type of work planned for the day.

The best of these cowboys will be well mounted and their equipment will be in good shape. They will know the lay of the pastures, the temperament of the cattle, and the roundup strategy. Once they are given the general orders for the roundup, they do not have to be coaxed or scolded or corrected. They know what has to be done and they will do it. As a rule, cowboys draw poor wages, but they are fiercely proud and independent and highly competent in their work.

Gathering cattle out of a big pasture resembles in many ways a military maneuver. Sometimes stealth and cunning are required, other times the speed and agility of the horses are the deciding factors. If all goes well, the herd will be surrounded, thrown together, and driven toward the working pens, and the outlaw cows will be foiled in their attempts to break back into the brush or to make a run for the hills.

At the pens, the cows and calves are separated and the calves are worked: branded, ear-marked, vaccinated, dehorned, and the bull calves castrated. The castrated males, or steers, are the basic meat-producing animals in the cattle industry, since they possess qualities of temperament and body conformation that make them superior both to bulls and heifers. At the spring branding, the calves may be roped and dragged to the branding fire in much the same way they were worked seventy or eighty years ago, or they may be run through a chute or calf cradle, a device that confines them while they are worked.

With the spring branding over, the rancher turns his attention to the summer jobs. There will be a number of odd jobs that have been put off until now: building and repairing miles of barbed wire fence, painting outbuildings, fixing corrals, keeping up roads through the ranch, prowling pastures and checking cattle, and patching leaky water tanks. But the most important task during the hot, dry months of summer is checking windmills and making sure the cattle have a supply of water. On a hot day, a cow may consume twenty-five gallons of water, and deprived of it for just a few days, she will die.

With the approach of fall, the rancher begins to think about shipping day, the day when all the calves on the ranch are loaded on trucks and sent to market. (The cows, or adult breeding females, are not sold. Only their offspring, which will usually weigh between 325 and 450 pounds, go to market.) Shipping day normally falls sometime between September 15 and November 15, depending on the price of cattle, range conditions, and other factors. When the calves are shipped, the cows are relieved of the burden of providing milk for them and begin gaining weight. The rancher hopes that his cows will be fat and in good shape before cold weather hits, as they will tolerate the winter better if they are fat.

If the calf crop brings a good price, the rancher will have a good year. But if the market is low, as it was between 1974 and 1977, then he must tighten his belt and hope conditions will be better next year. If he hits three or four bad years in a row, then he must also hope that he has an understanding banker. If he doesn't, he may be out of business.

And with the approach of winter, the cycle begins again: feed run, spring roundup, summer work, and shipping time, following the seasons in a rhythm begun many years ago when cattle first came into this country.

Ranching is not just a job. If it were, not many people would be interested in it. The pay is poor; the risks high; the hours long; the work hard, dirty, and often dangerous; the survival conditions ranging from difficult to damned near impossible. It is a style, a tempo, an attitude.

They say there are two good reasons for going into ranching: basic stupidity and an incurable attachment to the ranching way of life. Most ranchers I know freely admit to the first, but are also hooked on the second. Today they will tell you it is a blessing. Tomorrow they will not be so sure. It will probably depend on what the weather does, and nobody in the Panhandle would dare predict the weather.

COWBOYS

3
BILL ELLZEY

While I was on the Crown Ranch, I probably had thirty or forty cowboys helping me at different times. Some of them were paid for their work. Others had swap-out arrangements with me. Still others came and rode with the roundup crews just because they enjoyed the work and the companionship.

Bill Ellzey was the first man to draw wages on the Crown Ranch while I was there. I met him in August 1971, when my wife, Kris, and I visited the Lawrence Ellzey family at their ranch on Wolf Creek southeast of Perryton, Texas. After spending the afternoon riding horses around the ranch, we returned to the house. As I walked in the back door, I saw a bearded young man with black hair and a tanned face. Mrs. Ellzey introduced me to her nephew Bill, who had been working on the ranch for six months. In February a bad blizzard had struck the Panhandle, and Bill, an engineering student at Texas Tech, had driven up to Perryton to help his Uncle Lawrence gather up his cattle.

The work had appealed to him and he had remained on the ranch, living in an old hired hand's house along the banks of Wolf Creek.

I liked Bill the minute I met him. He had an easy-going manner, and in his eyes I could see intelligence, wit, and curiosity. He was a cowboy who wanted to become a professional outdoor photographer, and I was a cowboy who hoped to become a professional writer, and we had a lot to talk about.

Several months before this first meeting with Bill, I had gotten an idea for a writing project. I had learned that virtually nothing had been written about the Canadian River valley in the northeastern Panhandle, a wild and magnificent stretch of country that had always fascinated me. I didn't know why it had been overlooked, but I wanted to do a book on it—not a straight history or a rehash of the primary sources, but one that captured the sweep of the country and the stories of the people who had lived there. I wanted to do with the Canadian River something similar to what John Graves had done with the Brazos in his *Goodbye to a River*. After doing his research and interviews, Graves had made a canoe trip down the Brazos, and had used the trip as a kind of narrative thread throughout the book.

It struck me as the right approach to the Canadian, but since this was horseback country—and since you couldn't float a canoe in the shallow Canadian anyway—I thought it would be appropriate to make the trip a-horseback. And I wanted to take a photographer along, a man who had a feel for the country, who was competent in his medium, and who could handle himself and his horse in wild country.

Ten minutes after I met Bill Ellzey, I knew that he and I would make that trip together. Nine months later, in June of 1972, Bill's cousin Steve Ellzey hauled us, two horses, and a pack mule to the old ghost town of Plemons and we set out on a fifteen-day, 140-mile trip down the river. Bill

Bill Ellzey, cowboy and western photographer.

proved a perfect companion on such a journey, for while he was sensitive to beauty and had the eye of an artist, he was also tough enough to endure the hardships we encountered and cowboy enough to make the trip on a green-broke horse that pitched him off twice out in the middle of nowhere. He made a hand.

By the time I took the job on the Crown Ranch in 1974, Bill had retired from active cowboying and was spending most of his time on photography. But he was still doing some free-lance cowboy work on the side, so I called him up and asked if he would spend a few days with me on the Crown Ranch and help me settle into the job. While Kris stayed in Perryton and prepared for our move to Oklahoma, I planned to work on the ranch and batch until she could join me, and I thought it would be good to have Bill around if I needed some help and advice.

On January 8 I picked up Bill and his horse down on Wolf Creek and we drove up to the ranch. The day was a chilly thirty-five degrees, but the weatherman was predicting a high of sixty for the next day, and I figured we could saddle Suds and Dollarbill and ride from one end of the ranch to the other. I wanted to check out the windmills and fences and get a good look at the cattle. We left the horses in the corral with oats and hay, and moved our gear into a little hired hand's house south of the barn. For supper, we dug some steaks out of the deep freeze and opened a can of pork and beans. We stuffed ourselves on this bachelor fare and toasted my new adventure as a ranch manager. Tomorow we would feed the cattle and spend the rest of the day prowling around the ranch a-horseback.

The next morning when we looked out the window, we saw snow falling. A norther had moved in during the night, and the sixty-degree day the weatherman had promised had gone elsewhere. It was bitter cold outside, and over the next four days the temperature ranged from ten above to ten below zero. We never even saddled the horses.

In the mornings we fed the cattle, chopped the thick layer of ice that had formed on all the stock tanks, and thawed out windmills that had frozen up during the night. In the afternoons there wasn't much we could do except wait for the weather to break. We set up a cinder block in front of the barn and practiced our roping. Bill showed me the techniques he used in his basic head shot and also some horse loops he had learned from his father. When our hands grew numb with cold, we built a fire in a trash barrel and from time to time stopped to thaw them out over the flames.

One evening at sundown, when the temperature was near the zero mark and the air was perfectly still, we heard a chorus of coyotes tuning up out in the hills. They yipped and howled for two or three minutes, and we could hear them in all directions. By the time their howling reached a crescendo, it sounded as though we were completely surrounded by dozens of them. That was as mournful a sound as I had ever heard, and it made our little house seem warmer and brighter that night.

We waited four days for the weather to break. When it didn't, Bill said that he had to get back to his darkroom in Texas. We said good-by and he headed back down to Wolf Creek.

Over the next four years he returned many times to the Crown Ranch, sometimes as a paid cowboy and other times as a horseback photographer. In April 1974 he came up to help me with some pasture work, and we got ourselves into the wreck that I talk about in Chapter 13. And through it all, Bill Ellzey was, as the old timers on the boggy Canadian used to say, "a good man to ride the river with."

One winter day when Bill Ellzey was working on the LZ Ranch,
he drove up on this scene. A colt had gotten its foot hung in some
wire, and when darkness fell the coyotes had moved in. Ellzey
calls the picture "Wrong Step and Coyotes."

4
SANDY HAGAR

When we moved to the Crown Ranch, our nearest neighbors were two couples who lived on the YL Ranch, three miles down the road: Mark and Billie Mayo, and Sandy and Geneva Hagar. We had heard about them and knew where they lived, but I wanted to get settled into my job before I went calling on them.

After I had been on the ranch for about two weeks, I was driving home from the east pastures and took the county road that went right through the YL headquarters. If you approached the YL from the north, you drove through several miles of rolling sandhill pastures. The hills were covered with sagebrush and skunkbrush, the draws were dry and sandy, and there was not a single tree in sight. Then, a quarter mile north of YL headquarters, the vegetation in the big sand draw that ran parallel to the road changed abruptly. All at once trees appeared—not just a tree here and there, but a dense forest of hackberry, locust, and cottonwood in a strip a mile long and a hundred yards wide. On maps of Beaver County this draw is called

27

Timber Creek, and even though there is no active stream here, you can be sure that water is close to the surface. It was in this lovely wooded valley that Bob Maple, Mark Mayo's grandfather, established the headquarters for his ten-thousand-acre YL Ranch back in the 1890s.

When I first saw the place in 1974, Mark and Billie Mayo and their three children lived in a large two-story house (the original ranch house plus additions and improvements), and the Hagars lived in a small white house fifty yards to the north. East of Mark's house stood a magnificent red brick barn built in 1944, with seven horse stalls, a saddle room, and a grain room on the ground floor, and a hay loft on the second level. In front of the barn sprawled a set of working and shipping pens, and south of the pens were a milking barn, several hay sheds, and a small corral where Sandy kept his milk pen calves.

As I drove through the place, I saw a man walking toward me from the pens. He was a big-framed man, all bone and muscle and sinew without an ounce of fat. He walked with long, strong strides and kept his eyes fixed on the ground in front of him. I figured this must be Sandy, and now seemed as good a time as any to introduce myself to him. I stopped the pickup and rolled down the window. He didn't look at me until he was next to the pickup.

"Cold enough for you?" he asked in a booming baritone voice. I said yes, and told him who I was, though I was sure he already knew. "Sandy Hagar, pleased to meet you," he said, pulling off his right glove and handing me a huge paw. We shook, and I was glad that he didn't demonstrate the strength in that big hand.

We began making small talk about the weather and the cattle, but as we talked I noticed that Sandy's attention was shifting to the bed of my pickup. He was listening and carrying on his end of the conversation, but he was obviously more interested in seeing what kind of tools and litter I was carrying in the back. When he had seen all he

Sandy Hagar down at the milk pen at YL headquarters. Behind him is one of his two milk cows. Sandy, the ornery rascal, named this obviously feminine creature Ronald. At the left of the picture is one of the many milk pen calves he raised on a bucket.

wanted to see, he returned to the window and we continued talking. He never said a word about what he had observed, but I was convinced that Sandy Hagar had formed his first opinion of me, not on the strength of anything I had said, but on what he had seen in the pickup. I confess that it made me uncomfortable, even though I had nothing to hide or be ashamed of.

It would never have occurred to me to study the back end of a man's pickup, yet when I thought about it, it made sense. What a man carries tells you exactly what he's been doing for the past several days. You don't have to ask. The evidence is there on public display.

Later I learned why Sandy walked with his head down. He studied the ground in front of him. If any animal or human had passed through his territory, he knew about it. Driving around the ranch, he studied tire prints. If, on a snowy day, you made a foolish move, went into the ditch, got yourself stuck, and didn't want anybody to know about it, well, that was too bad. If Sandy came along, he would study the tracks, study the sign, and know exactly what had happened. He might not mention it for weeks, and you might think you had gotten away with it, but sooner or later he would get around to digging you about it. There wasn't much that went on in our little corner of the world that Sandy didn't know about.

He wasn't nosy or snoopy. He respected a man's privacy and had a keen sense of what was and wasn't someone's business. But if there were signs, he read them. If there was something in the bed of your pickup, he checked it out. He was a man who spent much of his time alone, and too much talk made him restless. He had his own ways of learning what he wanted to know. The old fox kept the bed of his own pickup swept out and as clean as a kitchen table.

Sandy and Geneva were born and raised in Lincoln County, Oklahoma, near the little town of Carney. Sandy farmed and worked on the railroad until he was laid off in 1960; then he moved to the Panhandle and went to work for Mark Mayo on the YL. The Hagars had raised two sons, Tony and David, and both boys had taken college degrees. At the time we met Sandy and Geneva, they were living alone. Now, you might have thought that Kris and I, both thirty years old and college educated, would not have had much in common with the Hagars, who were in their late fifties and had spent their entire lives in rural Oklahoma. But we had a great deal in common, and the Hagars became our close friends. Our differences in age, education, and background were not nearly as important as the other human qualities that bound us together. Sandy and Geneva were alert and alive, generous and warm, and they both had an earthy sense of humor.

Many a night during our four years on the Crown Ranch, when we got tired of looking at our four walls, we loaded up in the pickup and drove down the hill to visit Sandy and Geneva. In the spring of the year, Sandy and I often went walking in the timber north of his house, gathering wild poke salad. Sandy knew the woods and the plants that grew there. He taught me how to identify poke and when to harvest it, after a rain when the shoots were small and tender. In the summertime, we made ice cream. Geneva mixed up the ingredients, which included Sandy's fresh cream and milk, and Sandy operated the freezer, adding ice and livestock salt. Geneva's recipe yielded the richest, most heavenly vanilla ice cream I had ever tasted, and we consumed it in great quantities. On other summer evenings we opened a ripe watermelon and ate big slices out in the back yard.

On long, cold winter nights, we made popcorn. Geneva and Kris usually drifted into the living room, where they discussed Geneva's needlework and watched little Scottie as he crawled over the floor, while Sandy and I sat around the kitchen table, smoking Prince Albert cigarettes and discussing such weighty subjects as cattle, grass, weather, and work. It was on one of those winter nights, when the ladies were out of hearing range, that Sandy told me a yarn from his younger days in Lincoln County. Everyone was poor and entertainment often consisted of getting together and playing games. All the boys in town would get dates and take them to someone's house on a Saturday night.

On this particular night the kids played a kissing game. The girls went into one room and the boys into another. Between them was a door with a knothole in the middle. One of the boys would pucker up and put his lips into the hole, and a girl on the other side would kiss him and try to guess his name. A cat was purring peacefully on the floor on the boys' side, and some imp hatched a wicked plan. He seized the cat and placed its posterior against the hole in the door. "Okay," the boys called out. Some poor girl on the other side puckered up and planted a kiss on the cat. Then she stepped back and said, "Well, I do believe that's Mr. Billy Williams. He's the only boy who uses that nasty Star chewing tobacco."

Such was the level of Sandy's and my discourse on long winter evenings.

In the winter, after I had finished my feed run and started back to the house, I often stopped at the Hagars' house for coffee and conversation. Sandy was usually finishing his lunch, and when I banged on the door he would yell, "Come in, hammerhead." Around the kitchen table we drank coffee and discussed our work. For me, it served as a kind of seminar on ranch work. If I had encountered any problems on the Crown Ranch, I would bring them up and get Sandy's opinion of what I should do. A cow wasn't giving enough milk to support her calf. A bull was showing lice. A windmill had quit making water; did the problem lie in the leathers, the pipe, or the cylinder? A stock tank had rotted out along the bottom and had begun to leak. Sandy always seemed to know what to do.

A good deal of what I know today about windmill technology and livestock management I learned at the Hagars' kitchen table, while Sandy polished his plate with a biscuit or rolled a Prince Albert cigarette.

Mark Mayo, riding one of his Arabian mares, helps gather some Crown Ranch heifers. All at once he yells, "Buzzy-tail!" He has seen a rattlesnake.

5
MARK MAYO

Mark Mayo was many things. He was a shrewd, efficient ranch manager, a loyal friend, and a man who combined a cultivated intelligence with the common sense drawn from practical experience. But above all, he was a man-of-the-horse.

I remember the first time I ever rode horseback with Mark. It was in February or March of 1974. At that time the coyote population in our area was at a high point, and coyotes had killed and maimed several YL calves. (Some environmentalists argue that coyotes do not kill livestock, but live on carrion and small rodents. This is not true. A coyote that is old, lame, or for some other reason unable to provide for itself through hunting will turn to calf killing.) Mark, who had never been very fond of coyotes anyway, was in the mood for some Old Testament revenge. He was going to ride out some draws in his west pasture in hopes of finding coyotes, and he invited me to come along.

I saddled up Reno and Mark rode Saturf, his gray

Arabian stallion. Since he was going out to draw blood, he carried a Winchester .22 pump rifle in his saddle boot. After riding for several hours, we flushed a coyote out of a draw near the west end of the pasture. Immediately Mark spurred Saturf into a gallop and fell in behind the coyote. Then, with the stallion flying across rough terrain, Mark dallied the reins around the horn, whipped out the rifle, stood up in the stirrups, and commenced firing. The chase continued for half a mile or more, and at no time did Mark's hands touch the reins or the saddle. He guided Saturf with leg pressure, and somehow managed to stay aboard.

"This Mark Mayo," I said to myself, "is either a little bit crazy, or else he's something out of the ordinary a-horseback."

Several months later I watched Mark and Saturf perform again, this time in an arena at a horse show. Mark was demonstrating Saturf's jumping ability. Two bales of hay were set up in the arena, and Saturf jumped them handily. Then Mark pulled off the saddle and repeated the trick bareback. The crowd applauded, so Mark removed the bit and bridle. Controlling the stallion with nothing but leg pressure and voice commands, he cleared the barrier a third time—while holding a cup of coffee in his right hand.

Mark rode with the wild abandon of a Kiowa Indian, and this is not merely a colorful metaphor. He was the only cowboy or rancher I have ever known who actually preferred riding bareback to riding with a saddle. It was nothing for him to jump on Saturf and ride fifteen or twenty miles bareback, keeping the horse in a lope all the way. (Before the reader accuses Mark of cruelty to animals, I should point out that he rode desert Arabian horses, which are well known for their endurance; that he kept his horses in top condition; and that loping fifteen or twenty miles in an afternoon is nothing out of the ordinary for them.)

In my four years as Mark's neighbor, I had many

Mark was a man-of-the-horse. At a horse show in 1974 he jumped
Saturf, his Arabian stallion, over a barrier of hay bales—with no
saddle, no bridle, and holding a cup of coffee in his right hand.

occasions to ride with him, and often we rode bareback. I
did it enough to become fairly proficient at it, and to understand why Mark enjoyed it. Riding bareback, you feel
almost a part of the horse and experience a kind of wild
exhilaration that does not exist when there is a saddle
between man and beast. But you also experience pulled
groin muscles, battered gonads, and open sores on the legs
and posterior, which are aggravated by the accumulation of
horse sweat in your blue jeans. I rode bareback many times,
but I never acquired a taste for it, and I never understood
how Mark could endure the pain of it.

Mark's approach to horsemanship was highly unconventional, but so were his horses. His was one of the few
working cattle operations in the United States that used
nothing but Arabian horses. Over the years, ranch work
has become the exclusive province of the American quarter
horse, a breed that was developed especially for the demands of cattle work. The quarter horse offers great speed
over a short distance, enough size and strength to handle
grown cattle on the end of a rope, and that intangible
quality which often goes by the name "cow sense." These
qualities have made the quarter horse *the* general-service
horse in the West, and in ranch or rodeo circles, when you
speak of a horse, it is understood that you mean quarter
horse.

But on the YL Ranch, horse meant Arabian. Mark recognized and respected the good qualities of the quarter
horse, but he believed the Arabian had other qualities that
made it as good or better. He pointed out, for example, that
over four thousand years of desert warfare, Bedouin tribes-
men had bred into their horses such qualities as endurance,
soundness, and intelligence. Arabian horses, in their native
land, were tools of warfare, and as Mark often observed, "If
you want a good cowhorse, go find a good warhorse."

He broke and trained all his horses on the ranch. He
was a natural-born trainer who seemed to know instinc-

tively how to get the most out of every animal. By the time
the colt was two years old, when Mark put a snaffle bit in
his mouth and slipped on him bareback, the horse was
broke to ride before he even knew it. Rarely was there any
rodeo involved. Occasionally he would get piled by a
young horse, but that was the exception rather than the
rule.

He had an interesting and unusual approach to horse
training, one which was quite a departure from the old
spur-and-quirt approach of the Wild West. He believed
that, to get the maximum performance out of a horse, it was
essential that the horse like you, and that training a cowhorse was just a matter of communication—letting him
know what you wanted him to do. When Mark worked
with young horses, he showed tremendous patience and
used only token punishment.

I learned from experience that Mark's training techniques would not apply across the board to a different kind of
horse operation. I tried many of his methods on Crown
Ranch horses, and sometimes they worked and sometimes
they didn't. His methods grew out of his experience with
Arabians, which as a breed are known for their good disposition. They are affectionate, loyal, eager to please, and
fond of people. They responded to him and he responded
to them. On the YL Ranch, the temperaments of man and
horse had merged and had yielded a general attitude of harmony that reflected the best of both creatures. Mark really
enjoyed being Mark Mayo, and I think his horses really enjoyed being Mark Mayo's horses. Had one or the other
been taken out of context, they might have appeared
strange and unconventional. But in their native sandhills
north of the Beaver River, both were magnificent.

Tom Ellzey of the LZ Ranch in the Texas Panhandle, dressed for his winter feed run and in the company of his dog Sadie.

6
TOM ELLZEY

I can hardly remember the time when I didn't know Tom Ellzey. He and I both grew up in Perryton, Texas. We knew each other as children, and in high school we played football together (Tom as first-string fullback, I as a scrub) and participated in the same band and choir.

Tom was one of five children of Lawrence and Mary Francis Ellzey, and grew up on the six-thousand-acre LZ Ranch on Wolf Creek, southeast of Perryton. Since he was the next-to-oldest child, he never thought he would be able to return to the ranch and make it his life's work. The ranch was not big enough to support all the children, and so when he finished high school and left home, he set out to get an education and to find another profession.

He took a B.A. from the University of Texas in 1965 and a master's in anthropology from the University of Michigan. At that point he considered studying for a doctorate in anthropology or applying to medical school. He still had many fond memories of his years on the ranch, but since he knew he could never go back, he tried not to think about it.

In 1972, while he was teaching in the anatomy department of the Medical College of Ohio at Toledo, he got a call from his father saying that his favorite saddle horse had been killed by lightning. He hadn't ridden the horse in years, and its death seemed a fitting symbol of a ranching past that could never be recovered.

Then, in 1973, several things happened. In the summer he married a Toledo girl, Janet Soviar, and in the fall they made a belated honeymoon trip back to Texas to visit the Ellzey family. At that time the cattle market was booming. Tom's father and brother were running about two thousand yearlings annually, and they had decided it was time to bring another man into the operation. When Tom heard this he asked more about it. Wheels were beginning to turn in his head.

But he still had one major hurdle to clear. His wife had been born and raised in Toledo. All her family and friends lived in the city, and there was abundant reason for assuming that she could never adjust to living on a ranch in the stark Texas Panhandle.

He said nothing about the opening at the ranch until they were back in Toledo, and then he broached the subject with cunning: "Honey, do you remember how much you liked that cute little house on the ranch? How would you like to live there?" Janet said she would give it a try, and in November Tom resigned his job at the Medical College and they moved to Texas.

Tom, of course, had neglected to tell her that the "cute little house" in which he and his father before him had been raised was not insulated, and that the windows leaked cold air in the winter. But imagination and desire conquered these problems. That winter Janet hung blankets over the north windows, and the following year Tom put up storm windows and installed a friendly wood-burning stove.

So, at the age of thirty-one, after spending years reading books and taking examinations, dissecting cadavers and analyzing the bones of Maya Indians, Tom found himself back on the ranch. After living in cities for thirteen years, he could appreciate the ranching way of life. Getting on a horse and working with his hands again were very satisfying.

At the same time, Janet was making adjustments to her new life. She missed her family back in Toledo, and she found it hard to appreciate Tom's aroma when he came home after a day in the cow lot. But she had made up her mind to become a ranch wife, and before long she was riding a horse, building fence, driving a tractor, and feeding cattle.

In Tom's first year back on the ranch, an incident occurred which reminded him, if he needed reminding, that ranching wasn't all pretty sunsets and fresh air. He was out riding pastures one day and looking over a set of yearling steers. He was mounted on a horse named Rusty, a stout sorrel that was about half bronc. He noticed a steer that didn't look right, and as he rode closer he saw that it had pinkeye in both eyes and was stone blind. He decided that he had better take the calf to the home corrals and doctor his eyes. The calf wouldn't drive, so Tom took down his rope, gave chase, and dropped a loop around his neck.

Now, the cowboys on Wolf Creek have always been "hard and fast" men, which means that they keep the home-end of their catch ropes tied hard and fast to the saddle horn. I have heard Tom's father say that, back in his younger days, cowboys along the creek considered this a matter of pride. They were aware of the "dally" technique (winding the home-end of the rope around the horn after the animal is caught), but they rarely used it. The dally was all right for cowboys who worked in brush or timber and who might need to let their ropes go in a tight spot. But Wolf Creek cowboys worked on the prairie, and they tied solid. The dally was safer, but these Panhandle cowboys were a daring bunch and they weren't worried about danger—even though Tom's great uncle Frank Ellzey had been killed in a roping accident in 1917, when a horse he had roped jerked him and his mount into a tree.

Tying hard and fast is a time-honored and perfectly legitimate roping technique. Calf ropers in rodeo have always tied solid. Most of the old-time cowboys alive today rode and roped all their lives tied solid, and probably scoffed at anyone who didn't. Lawrence Ellzey tied solid all his life, and roped everything from baby calves in a branding pen to grown cows out on the range. That was the tradition Tom grew up in, and it was only natural that he had his rope tied to the horn.

So he roped the blind steer and was trying to get him headed toward the house. Now, a calf with two good eyes will naturally run away from a horse, but one that is blind is unpredictable. He might go anywhere. Before Tom knew what was happening, the blind calf had cut back on him and run under Rusty's belly. When the rope went tight, the bronc in Rusty came boiling to the surface. He went berserk and started bucking. Every time he bucked, the rope pulled tight against his legs and belly.

In this kind of storm, a cowboy has three options: he can try to stay aboard and get control of his horse; he can whip out his pocket knife and cut the rope; or he can bail off and try to get away from horse, calf, and that deadly rope between them. Of course this is highly theoretical. When a wreck comes, it comes quickly and the cowboy often has no time to think or act. His fate passes out of his hands.

Tom stayed with the horse as long as he could, while a little voice in the back of his mind was asking, "What are you going to do now, son?" And then Rusty put him away. When he hit the ground, he may have thought he was through for the day and had gotten out of the storm in good fashion. Then he felt the rope close around his ankle. He

was roped, just the same as the calf, and Rusty was dragging them both. And to make matters worse, he was tied up
so close to the horse that Rusty was kicking him every time
he took a step.

Off they went across the pasture. Rusty was completely out of control, bucking and dragging Tom and the
calf. I would imagine that Tom thought his chips had just
been called in and that he was going to join Uncle Frank on
the big ranch in the sky.

But finally his leg came out of the rope and he rolled to
a stop. He was beaten to a pulp, had rope burns, bruises,
and skid marks all over his body, but he was alive and un-
broken. (Anyone but an Ellzey would have been killed
three times. A strong and hardy breed, they are harder to
kill off than roaches.) He jacked himself up and hobbled
home. Later, he found Rusty in a far corner of the pasture.
He had dragged the calf to death, the saddle had gone
under his belly and he had done it some damage, and the
inside of his back legs was badly burned by the rope.

Tom moved to the LZ Ranch about the same time I
took the job on the Crown Ranch, and since we were old
friends and enjoyed working together, and since we were
only sixty miles apart, we made a swap-out arrangement.
He rode in almost every roundup I held on the Crown
Ranch and always served with distinction. He was fearless
and knowledgeable and as strong as a bull, and whenever
old Tom took a job or a position in a roundup, I stopped
worrying about it. In return, I went down to the LZ Ranch
to help with their roundups and cattle work.

In the summer of 1977 our swap-out arrangement took
a slightly different form. Up until then, we had traded out
only cowboy work, but in May of that year Tom mentioned that he needed some help hauling in and stacking
five cuttings of irrigated alfalfa hay. He wondered if there
might be some way of extending the swap-out deal to in-
clude that.

Now, any cowboy worth his spurs will begin walking backward at the first mention of hay, and the really good ones will run. Not only can you not ride a horse or swing a rope on a hay crew, but you might have to break a sweat. My initial reaction was to decline the invitation and scram, and had the invitation come from anyone else, I most certainly would have. But I had a great affection for Tom and his family, and I enjoyed working with them. As perverse as it may sound, the harder the work, the better I liked it. The Ellzey family was remarkable in this way. They worked very hard on their ranch, but they had a way of transforming the lowest forms of grunting manual labor into something else. I won't say it was fun, but it was something close to it.

So Tom and I worked out an arrangement. I would help him in the hay field, and he would pay the Crown Ranch for my time with alfalfa hay, which we needed and would have had to buy anyway.

At seven o'clock in the morning, Tom, Jeff Knighton (who was working on the ranch that summer), and I would climb onto the flat bed of the Ellzeys' bobtail truck, strap on our hay chaps, and pick up our hay hooks. Tom's sister Jill would start driving through the field, following the seemingly endless line of bales and picking them up with the pop-up side loader, which carried the bales up to the bed of the truck. When we had finished the load, we drove a mile west and put the hay into stacks behind Tom's house.

The mornings were not too bad, but after lunch we began to suffer from the heat. We stripped off our shirts and tied bandannas around our heads to keep the sweat from pouring into our eyes. We loaded and unloaded, hauled and stacked. In this type of work, you sweat so much that dehydration becomes a major concern. Often we grew dizzy and weak. Water did not seem to help, for while we consumed large quantities of it, it only made us nauseous and did not

Hauling alfalfa hay on the LZ Ranch. Tom Ellzey is driving, Jeff Knighton sits in a stupor on the shotgun side, and what's left of John Erickson rides on the running board. On the other running board is Nathan Ellzey, Tom's son. In a few years he won't be smiling when he leaves the hay field.

quench our constant thirst. Through trial and error we
finally hit upon a method of maintaining our body chemistry and controlling dehydration, one which had been used
by marathon runners who faced the same problem. Between trips to the field, we drank Gatorade (a thirst quencher that replaced salts and minerals lost in perspiration)
and beer, and very little water.

Along about five o'clock in the afternoon, when we
were so sore and exhausted we wanted to drop in our
tracks, we kept ourselves going with nothing but pride and
stubbornness and will power. We taunted each other. We
teased. We invented and bellowed lunatic songs at the top
of our lungs. I offer the following as an example of our dog-
gerel. This verse, one of many which sprang from our
fogged brains, celebrated the villain for whom we were
working, ranch owner and "trail boss" Lawrence Ellzey:

> The trail boss's orders inspire us with fear.
> He don't pay no wages but he furnishes beer.
> Two six-packs a month and a kick in the rear,
> Yippie-ti-yi-yo, what am I doin' here?

After spending two or three days in the Ellzey hay
field, I returned home and spent the next two or three days
recovering. The day after, I always felt sore and weak. The
skin on my hands and fingers had gone from blisters to
open sores. Every muscle and joint ached. My poor body
chemistry, robbed of salt and minerals and then deluged by
torrents of beer and thirst quencher, struggled to regain its
proper balance. Then, three weeks later, Tom would call
again. He had baled up another cutting. It was waiting in
the field.

"I'll meet you in the field at seven tomorrow morning," I would say, and as I hung up the phone, the words of
our hay-hauling song would echo in my head:

"Yippie ti-yi-yo, what am I doin' here?"

7
PREACHER HARDY

In 1974 when Kris and I visited the First Methodist Church in Beaver, I got my first look at Reverend Darrell Hardy. He was a tall, handsome, well-built man with graying hair and a pair of piercing blue-gray eyes. After the service, as we filed out the back door, we introduced ourselves to Reverend Hardy and his wife, Winonna. He already knew who I was, and he knew that I managed a ranch.

As we shook hands, he said, "John, if you ever need any help at roundup time, give me a call. I'd like to come out and make a hand."

"All right, Reverend Hardy, I'll sure do that." I smiled and tried to slip on out the door.

He gripped my hand and didn't let me go. I looked back into his steel-blue eyes. "I'm not kidding," he said.

Well, it was nice of him to offer his services, but with wild cattle and wild horses on the ranch, I figured I had all the problems I could handle. I didn't need a greenhorn rid-

Preacher Hardy on Sorrel, sorting cattle at a Crown Ranch roundup.

ing on my roundup crew. Reverend Hardy could take care
of the preaching and I would take care of the cattle.

Then, in the fall of 1974, I rode on a roundup crew on
the McFarland Ranch. The McFarlands joined us on the
west and were our neighbors, and we traded help at
roundup times. Reverend Hardy was there, too, only now
he was a-horseback and wearing a battered felt hat, a
leather vest, chaps, and spurs. For the next two or three
days, while we rounded up pastures and shipped cattle, I
had the opportunity to observe him at work outside his
church. He was good. He knew how to handle a horse, he
understood cattle, and he was afraid of nothing. The cowboys respected him, and everyone just called him Preacher.

The following spring, when I started putting together
a roundup crew, Preacher got an invitation, and from then
on he was one of my regular cowboys. The first time he
came out, he didn't draw any wages. I watched him.
Thereafter, he was paid the same as the other hands. I
knew that he would have worked for nothing, but I figured
if he was good, he ought to draw a check.

Preacher Hardy was raised on a farm south of Laverne
in Harper County, Oklahoma. In high school he played
football and basketball and broke horses in his spare time to
make spending money. After marrying his high school
sweetheart, he went to work in the oil fields in the Texas
and Oklahoma panhandles. He had worked himself into a
responsible position and was making a good living for his
wife and three small children, when he felt that he had been
called to the ministry. With the help of his wife, he finished
college and completed his work for the ministerial degree.
For six months before he took his first church in 1960,
he read the entire Old and New Testaments aloud to
Winonna, who corrected his pronunciation and gave him
gentle criticism.

After serving churches at Altus and Lawton, Oklahoma, he was called to the Methodist church in Beaver.

There, the Legend of Preacher Hardy began, and the people of Beaver County soon learned that his ministry would not be a quiet affair. Shortly after he hit town, he was riding on the McFarlands' roundup crew.

His first year in the community, someone dared him to ride a bull in the local rodeo. When rodeo night came, the announcer informed the crowd that the new Methodist minister would ride a bull in exhibition. It was a short ride. Preacher was blown out of his bull rope and given some flying lessons. Well, everyone thought, that was the end of that. The next night, Preacher Hardy climbed on another bull, and this time he was determined to ride him. His hand had come out of the rope the night before, and this time he took an extra wrap. It is sometimes called the "suicide knot," since if the rider is thrown, his hand may not come out of the rigging.

Out came the bull, bucking and twisting. Preacher rode him through several jumps, then went over the side. His right hand hung in the rope. While his family, friends, and parishioners watched in horror, the bull dragged him around the arena. Most of the spectators thought they had just lost a good preacher, but the pickup men rode in and finally worked his hand out of the rope. Preacher walked away sadder but wiser, and he never rode a bull again—until the next rodeo.

In 1972 he heard that the clown had not shown up for a local junior rodeo, and so he volunteered for the job. "I started clowning rodeos," he told me, "because I thought the spectacle of a preacher fighting the bulls would draw a crowd for the kids."

It probably did, and if the crowd was the least bit anti-clerical, they must have been vastly entertained that first night. They saw one bull chase Preacher to the fence and another run right over him as he hit the dirt. But, as in the case of bull riding, he didn't quit.

He clowned rodeos for years while he lived in Beaver,

and though he had some close calls, he was never seriously hurt by a bull. His worst injury as a clown occurred at a rodeo in Meade, Kansas, when the mule he rode as part of his clown act threw him into a fence and wrapped his body around a concrete corner post. He lay on the ground for ten minutes, and as the ambulance entered the arena to haul him off, he got up and went on to face twenty-one bucking bulls.

Why would a nice small-town minister do such things? There were two answers to that question. The first was that Preacher Hardy was a man of tremendous physical energy and drive, and a quiet, sedentary life had never appealed to him. As he once told me, "I've always been a daredevil. I like excitement." The second answer was that he considered his active, physical side part of his ministry. He worked and sweated beside his church members in hay fields and cow lots. He took his religion into the rodeo arena and the branding pen. He was never pushy or preachy about his religion, and he never asked for special favors. He worked among common men, and they respected him.

In August 1976, Preacher was called to St. John's Methodist Church in Oklahoma City, the first urban church he had ever served. Several months later, word drifted back to Beaver County that the Preacher Hardy Legend was alive and well.

Preacher was in his office one day when a lady came in and told him that a teen-age boy had just stolen a purse out of her car while she was inside the church. She had caught him in the act and had told him to come with her to the church office, but he had ignored her and walked away.

Preacher had never had much use for a thief, and he listened to the story with mounting rage. His reaction was automatic and thoroughly in keeping with his character. He leaped up from the desk, charged out the door, chased the seventeen-year-old boy three blocks on foot, and collared him in a shopping center parking lot. When the boy refused to go back to the church and face the police, Preacher grabbed his arm, twisted it behind his back, and said, "All right, son, you have two choices. You can either go back and take your medicine, or I'll break your arm." The boy took one look at Preacher's wrathful face and decided he would rather take his chances with the police.

When Preacher Hardy moved to a big city church, he was making a professional advancement, but it forced some changes in his active style of living. He had no farmers or ranchers in his congregation. There were no more bulls to ride, no rodeos to clown. But every fall and spring he arranged his schedule so that he could join old Sorrel and take his place on the McFarland Ranch roundup crew.

In the summer of 1978 I was driving down a sandy road in an isolated part of Beaver County. I had spent the day riding pastures and doctoring cattle, and was on my way home. A car approached from the other direction, and as it drew closer, I recognized the driver. It was Preacher Hardy. He had come to Beaver County for a short visit and had gone calling on some friends in the country.

We got out and shook hands in the middle of the road. Preacher was wearing a suit and tie, and there was a little more gray in his hair, but he looked as strong and vigorous as ever. We talked about old times and mutual friends, and he told me about his new grandbaby. Then, gazing off at the heat waves shimmering on the prairie, this clergyman, this grandfather, this irrepressible gray-headed cowboy-preacher made an astounding confession: "You know, John, I've been thinking about something for a long time. You might think I'm crazy, but I've always wanted to ride a bareback bronc, and when the Beaver rodeo comes around in the spring . . . ."

ROUNDUPS

8
SPRING ROUNDUP

In the Oklahoma Panhandle the first frost usually comes around the middle of October, and with it come the signs and smells and colors of approaching winter. The grass turns brown and goes to sleep. The skunkbrush and wild plum shed their leaves. The sagebrush becomes bare and brittle. For the next six months, a cowboy in this part of the country adjusts the rhythm of his life to short days and long nights, protects himself from the cold, and attends to the chores that must be done to keep the ranch running.

Then, sometime near the middle or end of March, the temperature climbs up into the seventies. The afternoons are longer now, and toward sundown you can hear the prairie chickens clucking on their booming grounds. The horses begin to shed their winter coats. Spring is in the air. And then comes the day when, in the stillness of morning, you fill your lungs with fresh damp air and you smell green grass. I can't describe the smell, but I believe that any cow-boy who gets that scent in his nostrils can tell you what it

57

means: spring roundup season isn't far away. It's time to
trim up the horses' hooves, grease the stock trailer, check
cinches and curb straps, get bridles, reins, and chaps oiled
and ready for work.

To anyone who loves the cowboy's life, this is the
most exciting time of year. A spring roundup and branding
is a time of work, but it is also a social occasion, when cowboys from several ranches get together after a long winter
and talk about their favorite subjects: cattle, horses, saddles, roping, weather, and, occasionally, a scandal or two
that has surfaced in town.

It is also a parade of sartorial splendor. Cowboys have
always been afflicted with a particular kind of vanity, and
since they cannot appear in costume at such respectable
functions as an Easter Sunday church service or the annual
band concert, they go to a spring roundup ready to strut.
Perhaps this vanity is a common characteristic of men who
are intimately associated with horses. The Bedouin tribes-
men, mounted on their prancing Arabian horses, and the
Indians of the plains, who doted over their fleet little
ponies, both raised male peacockery to high levels.

The cowboy cannot afford the extravagance of a sheik
or a war chief, but he will find some way of expressing himself through his gear and clothes, even if it means that he
must eat peanut butter sandwiches for a month or two. He
may come to the spring roundup mounted on a new horse.
If the animal has famous bloodlines, good conformation
and markings, a good mouth and disposition, some cow
sense and roping sense, then he probably cost a minimum
of a thousand or fifteen hundred dollars. Or the cowboy
may be riding a new saddle with a big dally horn that has
been carefully wrapped with strips of rubber. The saddle
probably cost him five or six hundred dollars—unless it has
some hand tooling on it, and then it may have cost twice
that amount. Or maybe he will be sporting a new pair of
chaps (seventy-five to a hundred bucks) or a pair of spurs

This picture shows the author in battle dress on a roundup morning. He carries a slicker behind the cantle of the saddle. Suds is equipped for roping (back cinch and breast strap). The high-top, high-heeled boots are made especially for riding. The author wears a pair of antique spurs fitted with spur straps that were hand-tooled by Tom Ellzey, and he has built a loop in his medium-lay nylon rope.

that he saw in a catalogue and just couldn't resist. Or maybe he'll be wearing a pair of new boots or carrying a new taffy-smooth nylon rope.

If he has won any trophies in the roping or rodeo arena, they will be on display: a prize buckle, a pair of engraved spurs, a trophy saddle. He won't have to talk about these items or point them out. Cowboys have very sharp eyes for such details.

The one item that won't be new is his hat. A new hat is always a liability, a step backward instead of a step forward. It takes months of wear, sweat, dust, and rain to make a hat right. Like wine, cowboy hats improve with age. The Saturday night cowboy in Austin, Texas, might strut across the dance floor in his new fifty-dollar Resistol and think he is right in style, but the working cowboy at a spring roundup wears a new hat without pride and with vague feelings of shame. A hat becomes as much a part of a cowboy as his nose and eyes, and the passing of an aged and cultured hat is mourned for months. Until he gets the hat broken in, he looks as though he had just had a haircut or a face lift. Something about him isn't right.

During roundup season, cowboys from several ranches often pool their manpower and move from one ranch to another until all the spring work is done. A cowboy may participate in roundups on four or five different ranches, each one of which may take from one to three days—or, on large outfits, several weeks. Since the work is strenuous and demanding of horseflesh, he may ride three, four, or five saddle horses and change mounts every day.

For me, a typical roundup day began at five o'clock in the morning. After putting on my boots and clothes, my first chore was to walk down to the barn and feed my horse some oats, so that he would have the strength and energy to make it through the long day. Returning to the house, I brewed a pot of coffee and ate a big breakfast of two eggs and a bloody steak. By the time the first pink streaks of day-

light were appearing in the east, I was at the barn saddling
my horse. I led my horse to the stock trailer and loaded
him, then went back to the barn to gather up my equipment: rope, chaps, spurs, and gloves. After closing up the
barn, I might pause to listen to the prairie chickens or to the
yipping of coyotes, and to drink in the lush spring air.
Then it was time to go.

As you approach the neighbors' ranch house, you see
other pickups and trailers parked on the side of the road.
The size of the roundup crew will depend on the size of the
pasture to be gathered, the number of cattle to be worked,
and the disposition of the cattle. Small pastures and gentle
cattle require less labor than large pastures and wild cattle.
An average crew in this part of the country usually has a
minimum of six or seven good hands, and sometimes as
many as fifteen. On a big crew, you may have some children, relatives, or friends who have come along for the
ride. They can carry out their assignments and ride out
their territory, but if the cattle are stormy, you can't depend on the green hands for much help. In a storm, you
look to that hard core of six or seven seasoned cowboys.
Working a roundup with a crew of experienced cowboys is
a delight. These fellows are professionals, and they possess
skills and qualities that set them apart from other men.

When all the roundup crew has arrived, a line of
pickup and trailer rigs pulls away from headquarters and
follows the boss to the point in the pasture where the
roundup will begin, which may be several miles away.
Back in the old days, the trip to the pasture was made
a-horseback and often took an hour or more. Pickups and
stock trailers have not only made this task more convenient,
but have greatly increased the mobility of a roundup crew,
while saving the horses for the actual work. On the negative side, there are many old-timers who will argue that
modern ranch horses are not as good as those of former
times because they spend too much time in a trailer.

At some point, either at headquarters or in the pasture, the boss will outline his strategy for gathering the pasture. In most instances the basic strategy is the same year after year, since ranchers are reluctant to change a plan of battle that has worked in the past. The strategy is determined by three factors: the size and shape of the pasture, the nature of this particular bunch of cattle, and the quality of the crew. The shape of the pasture is a constant and does not change from one roundup to another. The boss must take into account the kind of terrain (sandhills, flats, canyons, heavy brush) and the location of the pens, and he will distribute the crew where he thinks they will be needed. The disposition of the cattle is also fairly constant. Some herds are harder to handle than others. Over the years they establish habits and patterns, and the boss takes this into consideration.

The composition and quality of the crew is not constant, and may vary considerably from one roundup to another. Time conflicts are inevitable, even at such a festive occasion as a spring roundup, and the loss of a few good hands can mean the difference between a good crew and one that is adequate—if all goes well. The roundup boss knows his troops, their experience and knowledge of the pasture, and will assign the most demanding positions to those in whom he has the most trust.

But cowboys are only half the crew. The other half consists in what they brought in their trailers: horses. Horses build up reputations, just as the cowboys do. The good ones are respected for their speed, endurance, sure feet, cow sense, roping ability, and, for lack of a better term, heart, which has to do with a horse's willingness to go hour after hour, enduring physical punishment and giving everything he has until he has nothing left. The roundup boss knows the horses just as he knows the riders, and he will try to place the best horses in critical positions where horseflesh may be the difference between a quick, efficient sweep of the pasture and a long, frustrating morning. He will usually split up the best horses. Instead of sending two or three good horses to one part of the pasture, he may send one good horse with one that is out of shape or one that is green. That way he will have at least one good horse in every part of the pasture. Since you never know where the cattle may break or where the storm may occur, this is a good strategy.

So, before the roundup ever begins, the boss has thought over his battle plan. He knows the temperament and habits of the cattle, and he knows the lay of the pasture. When he sees his crew, both riders and horses, he makes the last minute adjustments of his general strategy. He gives the orders, sending three riders here, three there, two here, and one there. The cowboys nod and ride off in different directions. They understand the basic strategy and the part they will play in it. If all goes well, the plan will work. If someone makes a mistake or if the cattle happen to be in an evil humor, the strategy will be aborted, all previous orders will be suspended, and the success of the roundup will depend on the skill, good instincts, and courage of the cowboy crew, and on the physical ability of their mounts.

A roundup can be plotted only up to a certain point; then it becomes wholly unpredictable. If the boss knows he has fielded a good crew, he can relax and enjoyed the sport of a good roundup. If his crew is average, then he will be casting anxious glances at the points where cowboy savvy and horseflesh are thin, and he won't take an easy breath until the cattle are penned and the gate closed behind them. For better or for worse, once the crew has taken up their positions, the dice are thrown. Depending on what the cattle do, the dice may come up lucky seven or snake eyes.

9
A DAY ON THE YL RANCH

I always enjoyed working roundups on Mark Mayo's YL Ranch, and I especially enjoyed gathering his river pasture. The river pasture was something over four sections (four square miles, or about 2,500 acres). In the Deep South, eastern Oklahoma, or East Texas, a four-section pasture would be considered enormous. In New Mexico, Arizona Montana, or the Big Bend country of Texas, a pasture with four sections under one fence would be nothing out of the ordinary. In Beaver County, it was a large pasture.

And it was difficult to gather because of the terrain. On the north end you had high, brushy sandhills that extended southward to the flood plain of the Beaver River and joined a flat hay bottom about a quarter mile wide. The footing in the hills presented problems for a horse, not only because he was going up and down, up and down in soft sand that sapped him of energy, but also because he was confronted by sage, skunkbrush, and thorny wild plum thickets which he either had to hop over, go around, or plow through. On the south end of the pasture the terrain and problems were different. There, along and on both sides of the river, you encountered heavy stands of cotton-wood timber, dense plum and wild current thickets, and that most hateful variety of brush in these parts, the tama-rack.

The tamarack is an utterly useless form of vegetation that has moved into the plains country in the last forty or fifty years and has taken over some of the finest bottomland along the Beaver and South Canadian rivers. Old-timers have told me that the tamarack was not native to this re-gion, but came with settlers who planted them around their houses because they were hardy and could survive an un-friendly climate. In time, the seeds washed down to the river, sprouted, and sent their roots into the underground water that lies close to the surface. Subirrigated, the tama-rack thrived and multiplied, and today there are places along the Beaver River where a man cannot even crawl through the brush on his belly, much less ride a horse through it. Some ranches have been forced to bulldoze trails through the tamaracks so that a rider can cross the river and drive cattle from one side to the other. Gathering cattle out of tamaracks can be a horror. Cattle that are brush-wise behave like deer. At the first sound or sight of a rider, they will run for their sanctuaries and "brush up," standing motionless and hiding in the tamaracks until they are flushed out. Some will even lie down.

The tamaracks in Mark's river pasture were not as dense or as widespread as those on some ranches along the river, but they were bad enough to claw at a cowboy's face if he had to ride into them, and to provide brush-wise cows with a convenient sanctuary.

The river also presented a few problems. Rivers of the plains are as unpredictable as the weather. During a dry spell, the Beaver River may consist of a few pools of water sitting forlornly in a bed of dry sand, or its flow may be as

The two honchos of the YL outfit, Mark Mayo and Saturf, pause to repair some fence.

modest as that of a creek. But a rainy spell can transform
that dry sand into quicksand, and can send down a torrent
of water both wide and deep. If the river is up, the cowboys
assigned to the south side of the pasture must wade their
horses across and then convince the cattle on the other side
that they should cross over to the north bank.

So there is the pasture we're going to round up: four
square miles of sandhills, brush, timber, tamarack, quicksand, and water. Now what about the cattle? As a general
rule, Mark's cattle were gentle. They were especially easy
to work in a set of pens. The bulls were not particularly
nasty, and the cows weren't bad about kicking, fighting,
destroying gates, or trying to jump out of a pen. A good set
of Hereford cows, in other words. But they lived in a big
pasture with an abundance of hiding places, they possessed
any cow herd's natural resentment at being disturbed, and
on any given day and under the right set of circumstances
they were quite capable of testing the mettle of a cowboy
crew.

Which brings us to the final ingredient in the roundup
equation: the crew. For this roundup, which will be a com-
posite of the many occasions I helped gather that pasture,
we will have a crew of ten. Mark Mayo, the owner of the
ranch, will be riding Saturf. Meredith and Randy, his
daughter and son, will be riding Arabian mares, while
Steve, the oldest of the Mayo children and a student at Oklahoma State University, will be mounted on Shalime, a
handsome Arabian gelding with great speed and
endurance.

Bill Ellzey, the cowboy-photographer from Wolf Creek
in the Texas Panhandle, has come up to work the roundup
and will be riding his tall, gray quarter horse, Suds. Virgil
and Terry Dean from Beaver will be there, of course. Virgil hasn't missed a roundup on the YL in twenty-five years,
and his son Terry, age nineteen, has been riding with him
since he was about seven years old. Virgil will be mounted

on Sumbitch and Terry on Cowboy, both big, stout quarter horses. John Hesler, a banker from Beaver, has come out to make a hand. He'll be riding a horse named Skeeter.

Sandy Hagar, Mark's ranch foreman, won't be mounted but will drive the pickup and call the cattle. While the rest of us are getting them out of the brush and hills, Sandy will try to hold the herd around the pickup by throwing out a handful of cottonseed cake now and then.

I will be at the roundup too, riding Reno, the Crown Ranch's half-Arabian gelding.

We arrive at Mark's house around six-thirty on roundup morning. We have been up since five and are wide awake now. The air is fresh and damp, as it always seems to be on a roundup morning. We walk to the house and go inside. Some of the crew have already arrived and are drinking coffee. The others are on their way. No one will be late for a roundup, or if someone is, it will be for a good reason. We chat about the weather, and if Hesler is there, we give him some good-natured ribbing about his profession. I suppose only undertakers come in for more teasing than bankers.

Mark goes outside to load his horses, and the rest of us finish our coffee and head for our pickups. Five minutes later, Mark pulls away from the barn with his eighteen-foot gooseneck trailer, and three other pickup-trailer rigs fall in behind him. We drive a mile and a half south to the river pasture, then turn onto an oil field road and follow it another mile west. The end of the line is an oil well location. We park our rigs and unload the horses. We tighten our cinches, pull on our chaps, and buckle on our spurs.

Those of us who have rounded up this pasture before know Mark's general strategy. Instead of trying to gather the whole pasture in one bunch, we will gather the north end first, pen them, and then go to the south end and clean the river. Mark explains this to the new hands, explains that, in a big, rough pasture, it is easier to handle two bunches of 70 cows than one bunch of 140.

We will form a north-south line across the sandhills, push the cattle east, and gather them in a draw where Sandy will hold them with feed. When all the cattle are in, we'll move them south down the draw, bunch them at a windmill, and then start them toward the pens, a hundred yards to the east. Those of us who have worked this pasture before know that if there's a storm, it will occur at the windmill, where we must change the herd's direction from south to east. If the boys on the south end are late getting to the windmill, or if the cattle are moving at a faster pace than usual, there will be no one at the windmill to stop them, and they'll head straight for the river.

Mark, Virgil, Terry, and Hesler take the south end. Meredith, Steve, Bill Ellzey, and I take the north end. Randy will follow the oil field road.

We have formed a line a mile long across these high sandhills. It is imperative that we keep in line. If one rider gets too far ahead or behind the others, cattle can slip through and get behind us. If the north end gets too far ahead of the south end, we'll have cattle at the windmill before we have riders there to stop them. Timing and position are crucial. It is difficult to keep the line, because in this terrain, we can only see the riders to our immediate left and right. A cowboy who has worked in sandhills before knows what to do. About every five minutes, he rides to the top of a hill and stops. From this vantage point he can see the general outline of the roundup. If his end is too far ahead, he waits on the hill. The rest of the crew on his end see that he has stopped, and they stop too. On the other hand, if he leaves the hill in a hurry, we know that our end is behind and that we must ride hard to catch up. This is the way an experienced crew works. They don't yell or wave their hands. They simply watch the other riders and take their cues from them.

We move through the sandhills at a brisk pace, pushing the cattle to the east. As we approach the east fence line, a mile from the starting point, those of us on the north end increase our speed and change our direction from east to south. We can see Sandy's pickup in the draw now. He is calling the cows and holding them with cottonseed cake. He looks off to the south to see how things are progressing on that end. When one of the boys on the south end tops a sandhill to signal his position, and when Sandy determines that the timing is right and everything is going according to plan, he gets in the pickup and calls the herd down to the windmill. The noose is closing. So far so good.

But now we can see a problem developing. Our bunch of cattle is moving too fast. They're running down the sand draw toward the windmill, and the boys on the south end haven't come out of the hills yet to stop them. Bill Ellzey and I see what is coming, and we move out at a high lope. We anticipate one of two problems. If the fellows on the south don't make it to the windmill, Bill and I will have to get in front of the cattle and try to hold them. If the other cowboys do make it in time, their sudden appearance may startle the herd and they may try to make a run back into the sandhills to the west.

And that is what happens. Just as our cattle reach the windmill and have river on their mind, the cowboys come fogging out of the hills like the U.S. Cavalry. Their timing is just right. The old cows who had thought they were going to escape us and have clear sailing all the way to the tamaracks are suddenly faced with four belligerent cowboys mounted on good horses. Bewildered, they go into a mill. Blocked on the south, they come out of the mill headed west toward the hills. Bill and I are there waiting for them. We have taken the high ground on the other side of the draw because we know it is always easier to stop cattle when they are forced to run uphill. Suds and Reno, our horses, are prancing and snorting, just waiting for a relaxed rein and a touch of the spurs to give them the signal. They love it. The cattle are getting closer now, coming at a run. The two of us are facing a charge by seventy cows, but we

know that help is coming. Mark and Hesler are moving our
way.

We yell and wave our arms. We've got the advantage
with the high ground, and once again the old cows find
their escape route blocked. They glance to the left. They
see a hole and move toward it, but before they can take
three steps, Mark and Hesler are there, waving their ropes
and slapping their leggings. The cows mill and bawl. They
see another hole, take four steps, and find Virgil and Terry
waiting for them. They are captured. Their every thought
has been read, their every move anticipated, their every escape route blocked. They have attacked our lines and found
no weak spots, and with nothing else to do and no place to
go, they trot toward the pens.

We fall in behind them and keep them moving. As
they are funneling into the gate, a three-hundred-pound
heifer breaks and runs. Virgil starts after the heifer. He
tries twice to head her back to the herd, and when she
doesn't turn, he takes down his nylon and builds a loop.
Sumbitch falls in behind the calf, catches up with her, and
puts Virgil in position for a throw. Virgil swings the loop
three times over his head, lays it out there as soft as a
feather, drops it over the calf's head, jerks slack, and dallies
up to the horn. A few minutes later the calf trots meekly
into the corral at the end of a nylon.

The sandhill cattle are penned, and we take a five-min-
ute break. We check our rigging, tighten cinches, and talk
about the job we just completed. No one comes right out
and says it, but we're proud of ourselves. We are a good
crew and we worked well together. Now Sandy comes by
with a partial sack of cottonseed cake and gives a piece to
every horse. I can't recall a single roundup in the river pasture when he didn't do this. It is a kind of ritual, a reward
for the horses. Then we ride down to the windmill and let
the horses drink and cool down. It is nine o'clock now and
the day is warming up. Those of us who have been wearing

jackets take them off and tie them behind our saddles. When the horses have finished drinking, we move out toward the river.

As we ride, Mark glances around at the crew and begins formulating his plan for gathering the river bunch. He notes that Virgil's horse has worked up a sweat. "How much horse do you have left, Virg?"

"Lots of horse," Virgil replies.

Mark nods and studies the condition of the other horses. "How about the rest of you? Anybody out of gas?" All the horses are holding up. Mark stops and the rest of us gather around him. "Virgil, why don't you take Terry and Hesler and Steve and work the river, just like always. Be sure and check the southeast corner. There were some cattle over there last week. I'll take Meredith and Randy with me to the west end and we'll ride out the timber. John, you and Bill clean these sandhills north of the river and push the cattle down to the hay meadow. Then come back and set up north of the windmill. I expect they'll try to break for the hills, so you two will have to stop them. Sandy will be down on the river with the pickup. Push all the cattle to him. We'll try to bunch them there or at the windmill. Any questions?"

Virgil and his crew ride off to the southeast. Mark and his group lope off to the west end. Bill and I stay behind and discuss our assignment. We have to clear out an area of sandhills north of the river, half a mile wide and a mile long. We have to cover the ground in a hurry and get back in time to take up our positions north of the gathering point. Once again, the timing is crucial.

We split up and lope west, encountering a few cows and calves grazing in the sink holes between the hills. When they see us, they turn and make a dash for the river. I ride to the top of a sandhill and stop to take a look at the country around me. Off to the north, something moves in a plum thicket. It could be a coyote or a deer. I ride over to check it out. As I draw closer, I see a cow hiding in the brush. No, not a cow but a past-yearling bull with horns. He carries no brand or earmark. Either he belongs to the neighbors or he is a calf we missed at the last two roundups.

I ride toward him, swinging around to the north so that he will run south toward the hay bottom. When he sees me, he explodes out of the brush, running west instead of south. Reno is ready, and when I give him a slack rein, he turns on that great acceleration of his and we are in hot pursuit. We go flying over sandhills and leaping over brush. My life is now in Reno's hands—or more accurately, in his feet. We are galloping over rough terrain, and if Reno misses a step and falls, we could have a wreck. But I have ridden many miles on old Reno, and he's never lost his feet. I have to trust him.

With Reno's speed, we catch up with the bull and try to turn him south. Instead, he stops, cuts behind us, and heads north. Reno stops, changes directions, tears up the sand, and off we go again. We get position on the bull and try to turn him. This time he stops and glares at us. He is panting. He's hot and doesn't want to move. I take down my rope, let out about six feet, and pop him on the nose with the honda. He bellows and shakes his head. I ride in again and pop him between the horns. This time he comes after us and hooks Reno in the chest with a horn. I ride a short distance away, dismount, and examine Reno's chest. The horn drew blood, but it is only a superficial wound. I climb back into the saddle and think about what I should do now.

The bull is hot and snuffy. He has no respect for a horse, and he's obviously an outlaw—that's why he's unbranded. He is determined to stay in the hills, and there is no way I can drive him out. I can rope him, but Reno isn't stout enough to drag an animal this size through a quarter mile of sand. I would like to get revenge on him for hooking Reno and teach him some manners, but I don't like the odds: one man and one horse against a bull on the prod in the middle of sandhills—no thank you. And anyway, I don't have time to mess with him. Bill and I have to get back into position. So I spit tobacco juice in the bull's face and ride on.

Bill and I clear the sandhills and hurry back to take up our positions north of the windmill. From there we can see how the roundup is progressing. Virgil and his boys are moving up the river from the east. Meredith and Randy are pushing the cattle eastward across the hay meadow. On the south side of the river, Mark is bringing in about ten cows and driving them to a crossing. Sandy is stationed down by the river, standing in the back of the pickup and calling the cows to feed. His big voice carries a great distance in the quiet morning air: "Hyo! Skeffer! Succow! Hyo!"

Bill and I watch and wait. I am feeling apprehensive. I have been in this position before, and I know what is coming. When the cattle are bunched and the two crews on the river join up and start pushing the herd north, they will come at Bill and me at a run and the two of us will have to stop them. I have never been very comfortable with odds of thirty-five to one. A herd of charging cattle bears an unpleasant resemblance to an army of blood-thirsty Comanches bent on taking some cowboy scalps. Sometimes you can stop such a charge, and sometimes you can't. If you can't, and if the herd is spilled into the hills, you will be haunted by the feeling that in a tight spot you choked, made a foolish decision, or simply lacked the skill to get the job done. We wait, nervous and impatient.

Reno is calm. He is watching the cattle below. He knows what is coming and he isn't worried about it. I'm riding a good horse. I'm working with a good hand in Bill Ellzey, and he is well mounted on Suds. If we can't stop the charge, it can't be stopped. Bring those cattle and let them try to break for the hills!

Most of the cattle are in now. Virgil and his boys are

flushing a few cows out of the tamaracks, and Mark is
bringing back a cow and calf that tried to sneak across the
river. Sandy has started the pickup and is driving toward
the windmill, calling the cows to get them to follow. The
herd starts moving north, kicking up a cloud of red dust.
The bellowing of bulls, the bawling of cows and calves, the
whistles and shouts of the cowboys reach our ears. Above it
all we can still hear Sandy: "Hyo! Skeffer! Succow!"

The herd is stringing out now. The lead cows have
broken into a trot and are looking for daylight. They have
sandhills on their mind. Or, as Virgil would say, they're
ready to quit the country. They pass the pickup and keep
coming, gathering speed as they see the hills in front of
them. Bill and I wait quietly. We've got the high ground,
and we want to meet them when they are on an uphill pull.
It's a good battle plan, but the waiting puts our nerves on
edge.

We wait until the last possible moment, then we both
move forward to challenge the lead cows. We yell and wave
our arms. Confused, the first wave of cattle splits and
widens the front, which puts us at a disadvantage. We have
to ride hard now to cover more ground and to meet pressure on three or four points instead of just one. One old
cow puts her head up in the air and breaks for daylight. Bill
and Suds fill the hole and turn her back. On my side, two
cows and calves take aim at the hills. Reno pivots on his
hind legs and turns on the speed. When we head them off,
they try to cut behind us, but Reno plants his feet, reverses
his direction, and heads them again. He moves with such
force and quickness that I lose my right stirrup and have to
grab the horn to stay aboard. Reno is an explosive horse,
and I often find myself riding in peculiar positions.

Bill and I have stopped the charge on the north, while
the rest of the crew has driven the herd away from the
windmill and started them moving to the east. They begin
to string out now in a long line, with the more athletic cows

trotting out front—and still looking for a weak spot in our lines—and the slower cows bringing up the rear. Now we go into what might be called the basic configuration for moving cattle. Slow horses, old horses, green horses, and inexperienced riders move to the back of the herd and ride drag, where the primary task is to keep the herd moving along. The better horses and riders move to the flank and point positions. You want your best manpower and horse-flesh matched against the wildest, rankest, and most troublesome cows, who invariably find their way to the front of the herd.

A cowboy who is good enough to ride the point position on a cattle drive is proud of it. But if he isn't qualified to ride point, either because he lacks the horseflesh or because he isn't familiar with the pasture, the temperament of the cattle, or the route to the pens, then he had better move to the rear. I have removed myself from the point position on many occasions, sometimes because I knew I didn't have enough horse to do the job and other times because I was not confident that I knew where the cattle were likely to break for open country. The point man must know the pasture well enough to anticipate problems before they occur. He must know the habits of the cattle—how aggressive they are, when they should be slowed down and bunched, and where along the way they usually try to cause trouble. He must watch the other riders and know at all times where they are. His thinking must be at least one step ahead of the cattle. And if trouble develops, he must have enough horse under him to ride hard and fast.

One mark of a good professional cowboy crew is the absence of petty jealousy and rivalry among the hands. I think any cowboy would rather ride point than drag. The action takes place on the point position. That's where man and horse are put to the test. If you're crazy enough to attend a roundup, you're crazy enough to enjoy the competition, the speed and action that occur on the point position, that match-up between wild cows and good horses. But the best cowboys I have known were those who worked as members of a team and subordinated their own desires to the demands of the roundup. A good cowboy knows his limits and those of his horse, and when he finds himself in a position for which, on that particular day, he isn't qualified, he will give it up without being told or asked to do so. He will take a less glamorous position without complaint.

We have the herd stringing out in a long line and heading eastward. Everything is in good shape and we have shifted into our positions for the drive to the pens. The slower horses move to the rear and the more experienced horses and riders move to the flanks and points. As it turns out, I am in a natural position to take left point, which, in this pasture, is crucial. If the cattle break on the left point, the nearest fence that will stop them is a mile and a half away. I have never ridden left point in this pasture, but I feel I can handle the job today. I look back over my shoulder and locate Mark over on the right flank. He's the boss, and I don't want to take the point unless he thinks I'm ready for it. He's not watching me or riding up to take the point himself, so I know that he has told me to go ahead.

I nudge Reno and ride up to the head of the line. Virgil is on the other side riding right point. It is our job to control the lead cows and keep them moving in the right direction. Virgil will keep them from breaking back to the river, and I must prevent them from making a run for the sandhills. Today they are looking around. They want to make a run.

After moving the herd eastward half a mile, we come to a fence that angles off to the north. Here we will put the herd on the fence and change their direction from east to north. Cattle are peculiar beasts. For some reason, when you change their direction they want to run. I know this. I also know that at this point in the pasture the herd is strung out over two hundred yards, and that on past roundups when Mark was riding point, he slowed the herd down here and bunched them up for the final drive to the pens.

So I lope off to the north and station myself on a sandhill. Seeing no one on the point, the cattle in the lead break into a run down the fence. They soon learn that they have been outsmarted. Pouring down the fence, they look up and see me holding the high ground in front of them. Bill Ellzey is beside me now, and Mark is moving up from the rear to strengthen our position. We have captured them in a natural dish between two sandhills. On the right they are blocked by a barbed wire fence. On the left they face three stubborn cowboys on high ground. The run is over. The lead cows swish their tails and bawl, while the rest of the herd comes in from the south.

A herd that is bunched is easier to handle than one that is strung out over a long distance. With the cattle in one group, the crew can form a tighter line of defense. We want the cattle bunched when we start driving them toward the corral. So, when the drag comes in from the south and we have thrown the herd together, those of us on the point back off and the rest of the crew starts pushing the cattle northward again. Just another quarter mile and we will be at the pens.

Most of the cattle are hot and tired. The crew has dominated them from the start and has taught them some manners. They are moving slowly up the fence now, and those of us on the point begin to relax a little and talk about our experiences of the morning. But we have been on enough roundups to know that we can't allow ourselves to slip into carelessness. A roundup isn't over until the last animal is driven into the corral and the gate has been shut.

We move north through a grove of hackberry trees and then on to the windmill that stands a hundred yards southwest of the pens. Here the cattle swarm around the tank to get a drink. Thi is always a dangerous spot in the roundup. The cattle want to stop, but we must keep them moving. The longer they stand around the water, the greater the chances are that we will lose some of them. "All right," Mark yells, "let's hit 'em. Let's go!" The crew back on the drag begin to yell and swing their ropes, while the point riders form a line that will direct the cattle toward the pens. We are studying the bovine faces in the herd for cows that may have thoughts of making a break. The cows trot toward the pens. I lope out and stay beside the lead cow and keep her pointed toward the gate.

The lead cow has gone into the corral now, and the rest of the herd is strung out in a line back to the windmill. They are moving quietly, and unless someone gets careless, we should pen them without incident. Losing one cow out of a herd of eighty is no major disaster in itself. But cattle are motivated by a herd mentality. When one cow makes a run, there are twenty or thirty more who will try to follow. Cattle which, one minute, were moving quietly toward the pens can, the next minute, become as unruly as deer, and in a matter of minutes the entire morning's work can be lost in what is often referred to as a storm, a spill, a wreck, or a jackpot.

We are lucky this time. We push the last baby calf into the corral and shut the gate. We did it. The roundup is over.

Roundup action: Virgil Dean applies the crown brand while Preacher Hardy holds the front leg and Stephen Mayo holds the back. Terry Dean comes in with another calf on the string.

10
HELL ON NEIGHBORS

While I was managing the Crown Ranch, it was my job to organize three roundups every year. Around the middle of May we had our spring roundup to brand the calves. At the shipping roundup, which usually fell in late September or October, we gathered the pastures, sorted off the calves and cull cows, loaded them onto trucks, and sent them to market. Then in November or early December we rounded up again, branded the late calves, and cut all the cows and calves into one pasture for the winter.

My friend Tom Ellzey, a veteran of many gatherings on the Crown Ranch, once remarked that my roundups were never dull. That was a masterpiece of understated cowboy humor. Translated, it meant that my roundups were often rather wild affairs. You never knew what might happen on a Crown Ranch roundup, but you came prepared for the very worst. You brought your toughest horse, or if you didn't have one with a lot of endurance, you brought two. You came mentally prepared to do battle with the wildest cattle in four states. And before you climbed on your horse on roundup morning, you wanted to be sure that your health and life insurance premiums had been paid up, and that you were on good terms with the Lord.

If my roundups were not dull for the cowboys, they were not much fun for me. It was my job as the roundup boss to gather a crew and plot a strategy that would enable us to pen cattle whose cunning, speed, and temperament made them a formidable enemy. A mistake in planning could result in a wreck of major proportions, with cattle running in all directions, cowboys pursuing them by one's and two's on jaded horses, and the branding work either held up or called off for the day. In a world where hijackings and wars make the headlines, this doesn't sound like much of a problem. But to me, it was a matter of pride and principle. I wanted to gather the cattle in an orderly, professional manner, to work the calves, and be done with it. I didn't like sloppy work, especially if my name was associated with it. I wanted to do it right.

I feared the Crown-branded cattle, and I began dreading my spring roundup with the approach of warm weather—at the very time that I began looking forward to working roundups on the YL, LZ, and McFarland ranches. I began planning my roundups a month in advance, recalling the problems we had encountered the year before, studying the shape of the pastures, and rethinking my strategy. Two weeks before the roundup, I drew up a list of the crew I wanted and began calling. If it appeared that my crew would be thin, I had additional cause for worry. About a week before the roundup day, anxiety would begin to appear in my sleep, as night after night in my dreams I found myself on horseback, facing the charge of a hundred wild-eyed, stampeding cattle, and awoke in a cold sweat, reaching across the bed for a bridle rein.

Roundup morning found me tense and brittle, giving wooden responses to the carefree and lighthearted

comments of my friends on the cowboy crew. When we
mounted up and hit the pastures, I always felt as though I
were riding off to my own funeral. I could never relax until
we had driven those damnable cattle into a pen they
couldn't destroy and had closed the gate behind them.

The Crown Ranch cattle were a bunch of snakes, and
they would run at the first sight of a horse. When we
rounded up the west pasture, which was two miles long
and two miles wide, we very seldom got within two
hundred yards of a cow until we were halfway through the
roundup. The cattle on the north end would see us coming
and within seconds they would be heading south at a dead
run. Up ahead, we could see a line of cattle going through
the hills like a giant bullsnake.

Cattle set the tempo of a roundup. If they are gentle
and move slowly, the crew can handle them slowly and
gently. But if every step they take is in a run, then the crew
must respond in kind.

Our working pens were located on the north end of the
west pasture. Under normal conditions, the roundup
strategy would call for the crew to start the gather on the
south end, push everything north, and pen them. On the
Crown Ranch, conventional strategy did not work. The
cattle in the west pasture were so wild that we started the
gather on the north end, pushed everything south, bunched
them (or tried to) in the southeast corner, and then drove
them two miles north to the corrals. Had we started the
gather on the south end and tried to drive them directly to
the pens, I doubt that we could have handled them, even
with a big crew. We had to get the run out of them before
we could control them, driving them four miles instead of
two. And even using this ploy, we had some tense moments.

When we started through the pasture, the cattle
moved out so fast that we had to lope and gallop our horses
through the first mile and a half of the pasture just to keep

up with them. This gave the roundup the appearance of a
cavalry charge, and a stranger observing the procedure for
the first time might have thought we were a bunch of green,
possibly drunken cowboys making sport out of chousing
cattle. But we weren't chousing them, we were just trying
to keep them in sight, and for a very good reason. When
they hit the south fence and found their path blocked, they
did not slow down or stop, as any civilized cow brutes
would have done; they kept right on running in whatever
direction seemed most convenient, which might mean
north, east, west, or all three at once. We had to be there to
stop them, and in order to get there in time, we had to whip
and spur through two miles of hills and brush. When they
hit that south fence, they came roaring back like cannon-
balls.

This was the testing ground, and we could always
count on a major battle here. When the cattle came charging back, we had to throw up a line of cowboys and horses
(between seven and thirteen) to turn them. Usually they
made their run up the east fence line. Riding like
Comanches, the cowboys on the east side would charge
straight at the lead cows, yelling at the top of their lungs
and waving ropes and vests. If this maneuver succeeded,
the charge was turned to the west, where the other cowboys were waiting to turn them to the south. Our objective
was to put them into a mill and hold them until all the crew
came in from the west. When we reached full strength, we
moved toward them in a semicircle, tightening our grip on
the herd and giving them less running space.

Looking back, I'm astounded that we never lost the
herd at this point. We had plenty of scares, some furious
storms and wild dashes across the pasture, but we never
spilled the herd. This astounds me because the cattle tested
us every time, and they were dangerous enemies.

You might think that after this herd of cows had run
anywhere from half a mile to two miles through sandhills;

after they had hit the bottom of the pasture and tried to break back; after they had tested the skill of the cowboys and the endurance of the horses; after they had been stopped, milled, bunched, and gathered—after all that, you might think they would be ready to give up and walk the last two miles to the pens. Not these cattle. No matter how well we and our horses performed on roundup day, we were never able to dominate this cow herd. Each of us was aware that, at any point in the drive to the pens, we could lose them. It was as if we were transporting bombs and dynamite that could explode at any moment. We could never relax or become careless.

On the drive to the pens we always put three top cowboys and horses on the point, one to ride in front of the cattle to prevent them from running, and the other two to back him in case trouble developed. The point man got out in front of the herd when the drive started and he stayed there until we reached the pens. By the time he got there, he usually had a crick in his neck, since he had ridden two miles looking back over his shoulder.

What made the cattle so wild? I don't know. It may have had something to do with the way they were handled over the years, or it may have been a trait that was transmitted through the bloodlines of herd bulls used on the ranch. Both opinions were argued at one time or another by cowboys who helped on the ranch. All I can say is that wildness was in the cattle when I arrived on the ranch in 1974, and it was still there when I left four years later. In between, it gave me bad dreams.

In the spring of 1977 we gathered the middle pasture and brought the cattle to the pens. It was a typical roundup morning, which meant that we and the horses were tired and galled. We had fought a running battle with the cow herd and were ready for a rest. The way the home pens were set up, we pushed the cattle first into a wire trap (a trap is just a small holding pasture, in this case consisting of three or four acres), and then we drove them on into the corral. In the trap, the herd had fences on all sides and very little running space. In the past pushing them on into the corral had been a simple matter.

But on this occasion we put them into the trap through a gate on the south, they ran straight to the north end, tore down a wire gate, and poured right back into the pasture from which they had come. They did this so neatly and efficiently that some of the cows didn't even have to break stride. We watched as our little animal friends thundered down a ravine and headed north in a high lope. Profanity filled the air. We pulled our hats down on our heads, popped our horses with spurs, and off we went on another tour of the pasture.

As it turned out, we were pretty lucky. Tom Ellzey and Jim Gregg galloped out and headed the cattle before they had gone too far. When they peeled them off the fence and turned them east, the rest of us were there to catch and hold them, and fifteen minutes after the wreck occurred we had them in the corral with a big iron gate closed behind them. Only then could we take a deep breath and talk about what a fine bunch of cowboys we were.

When I think of memorable roundups on the Crown Ranch, the spring roundup of 1975 comes to mind immediately. That year I assembled a large cowboy crew. A few of these hands were day help (free-lance cowboys who drew wages), but most were neighbors with whom I had worked out swap-out arrangements. On the first day of the roundup, we gathered the cattle out of the big east pasture and drove them to the middle pens, which were a small set of working pens a mile and a half from home. J. C. Rabe, one of my neighbors, had come over to help, and when we had the cattle penned, he walked through them to see if one of his cows had strayed into our pasture. While he moved through the herd checking earmarks and brands, the rest of us leaned against the fence and talked. Then, all at once, we heard what sounded like a rifle shot. Some of the crew began moving toward J. C., who had fallen to the ground. I walked over to see what was going on and arrived just in time to hear J. C. say, "I think she's busted."

While J. C. had been moving through the herd, a cow had kicked him, and the sound we had all heard was a leg bone breaking in half. The bone snapped right above his ankle, and to make matters worse, the joint was also dislocated. J. C. must have been in terrible pain. It showed on his face, which turned very pale, and there were times when he thought he was going to lose consciousness.

Preacher Hardy was on the crew that day, and he knew emergency first aid procedures. He went right to work on J. C. His first problem was to get the boot off before swelling set in, before the ankle got so big that the boot would have to be cut off. When he got it off, he called for a saddle blanket. One of the boys jerked the saddle off the nearest horse and brought the blanket. Preacher wrapped it around the leg to form a splint, and then he called for belts. Three or four of the hands whipped off their belts and handed them over, and Preacher buckled them around the splint.

By this time, Jimmy Smith, another neighbor whose pickup happened to be at the middle pens, brought up the pickup and cleared out the back end. Seven or eight cowboys lined up on both sides of J. C., put their hands under his body, and lifted his 230 pounds off the ground. As gently as possible they placed him in the back of the pickup. Preacher Hardy and Tom Ellzey got in the back to take care of J. C. on the way to town, and off they went on the twenty-mile trip into Beaver. Jimmy Smith drove slowly through the pasture, but he had to negotiate a rough, sandy road, and I'm sure the trip was none too pleasant for J. C. They delivered him to the hospital and

An old-fashioned roping roundup requires a big crew. Shown here are, from left, Jim Gregg, Tom Ellzey, Ron Sallaska (standing), Preacher Hardy, Terry Dean, John Ellzey (standing), Virgil Dean and Mark Mayo on horses, and Sandy Hagar.

left him under the care of Doc Calhoon. They made it back to the ranch just as the rest of the crew was finishing up at the dinner table.

J. C.'s accident dampened our spirits that day, but a broken leg was just one of those things that could happen around cattle. When we discussed it among ourselves, though, we found that not one of the cowboys on the crew had ever seen a bone broken at a roundup.

The next day the crew gathered at the Prairie Parthenon before daylight and we all had a cup of strong coffee. Several of us had visited J. C. at the hospital the night before, and we gave our reports. He was resting comfortably, but he had gotten a nasty break and would have to be transferred to a hospital in Norman, Oklahoma, where surgeons could pin the bone.

Around seven o'clock we went out in front of the house and prepared to gather the west pasture. Horses were led out of trailers, cinches were tightened, and the strategy was discussed. Jimmy Smith had brought a big black horse that morning. He was a nice-looking horse, but Jimmy hadn't ridden him much that spring and knew that he had a tendency to be "cold backed"—on a cool spring morning he might pitch. So Jimmy led the horse behind the pickup, up and down the road, to warm him up and get some of the kinks out of his back. Then he mounted up. The horse was still acting silly. Jimmy slapped him on the head and spurred him. The horse sulled and went down, pinning Jimmy's leg beneath his weight. The other boys came to his aid and got the horse back on his feet. Jimmy limped around for a while, said his leg was all right, and climbed back into the saddle.

We went on and rounded up the west pasture. Jimmy took the east side of the pasture and rode point on the way to the corrals. It was a typical gather, which means that Jimmy did some hard riding for the next hour and a half. He never left his position and never said a word about his leg. When we had penned the cattle, he came up to me and asked if I had enough crew to brand the calves without him. He had some things he needed to do. I said sure, and thanked him for his help. Again, he said nothing about his leg.

When he left the ranch, he drove straight to the Beaver hospital, to which he had hauled J. C. the day before. Doc Calhoon took an X-ray of his leg, checked him into the hospital, wheeled him off to the emergency room, set his broken leg, and put him in a cast that he carried around for the next two months.

Well, that evening I visited the hospital again, this time to look in on two of the neighbors, both in the same wing of the hospital, both with the same leg broken, and both under the care of Doc Calhoon. And of course both had gotten their broken bones at the same place—my spring roundup on the Crown Ranch. On one of my calls at the hospital, I caught Doc Calhoon out in the hall and asked if, in the future, he would pay me a commission on all the bone business I sent his way.

The next Sunday I attended services at the Beaver Methodist church. Preacher Hardy was in the pulpit, and when the time came to pray for the sick, he asked that we remember J. C. Rabe and Jimmy Smith in our prayers. I wanted to crawl under my pew and hide. I know it wasn't my fault that, in two days' time, two of my neighbors had gone to the hospital with broken legs, but I figured it didn't do much to enhance the reputation of the Crown Ranch.

I thought Virgil Dean put it very nicely. He hadn't attended the Broken Leg Roundup, but he had heard about it. When I saw him in Beaver a few days later, he grinned and said, "Boy, you're hell on neighbors, aren't you."

11
THE NORTH POLE ROUNDUPS

The Broken Leg Roundup of 1975 gave my cowboy friends plenty of ammunition for teasing me and giving me a hard time. The fall roundup of 1976 gave them more.

At the fall branding, we rounded up all the pastures, separated the dry cows from those with calves, and branded the calves. We put all the pairs into the middle pasture for the winter and split up the dries between the big east and the west pastures. I put the cows with calves into one pasture for two reasons. First, since lactating cows require more energy and protein supplement during the winter months, I could feed the wet cows in the middle pasture more supplement than the dry cows in the other pastures. This extra feed not only kept the cows in better shape, but also improved the condition of the calves. And second, in the event Keith Good and the trust committee at the Booker bank decided to sell the heavier calves in the spring, we would have them all together in one bunch and we would only have to gather one pasture.

In setting the date for the fall roundup, I tried to wait as long as possible without waiting too long. The longer I waited, the more calves we could brand at a young age, when the shock of branding, dehorning, and castrating was less severe than if it occurred when they were older. On the other hand, if I waited until too late in the season, I took the chance that we might run out of pretty weather. In these parts, winter often comes without warning. An early snow can make country roads difficult to travel, and a prolonged cold spell can take a lot of the fun out of riding horseback and working cattle. Sometimes cowboys are forced to do their work in nasty weather, but given a choice, they prefer a warm, sunny day.

In August 1976 we had a long spell of hot, breathless days. The grass was brown and dry, sandburs and goatheads were headed out and had become a plague, wasps droned in the still afternoon air, and windmills hardly turned at all. It was unbearably hot, and in the middle of the afternoon a cowboy felt a powerful urge to follow the example of any sensible cur—find a piece of shade and take a nap. That's the way I felt, anyway.

The first norther of the year blew in around the end of August, bringing cooler weather and the first signs of fall. By October the sandhill country was showing its autumn colors of brown, orange, yellow, and red. The first week of November gave us an example of glorious autumn weather, with warm days and cool nights and afternoons that were so still and silent you could hear trucks on the highway four or five miles away. That is the kind of weather you want for a fall branding. I got on the phone, called the crew, and set the date for November 11.

The day before the roundup I went about my preparations, setting out the branding heater and the irons, sharpening the dehorning tubes, and grooming my saddle horse. The temperature climbed into the eighties and I stripped down to my T-shirt. If anything, it was too warm, and I hoped that tomorrow would be a little cooler. It was.

Erickson pauses to tighten a spur strap while Suds catches his breath.

When I got out of bed at five o'clock on roundup morning, I heard the wind roaring outside. I knew it was a north wind. The Prairie Parthenon resembled a musical instrument in that it played a different tune with different kinds of wind. A north wind made the house moan and whistle, and that is what I heard as I stumbled through the dark house toward the coffee pot: a bunch of moaning and whistling. That was no ordinary breeze outside. It was a norther.

I pulled on my clothes and boots and went down to the barn to feed my horse. When I stepped around the corner of the house and caught the wind in my face, I gasped for breath. I went on down to the barn, did my chores, and hurried back for a cup of hot coffee. By the time I reached the house, the wind had cut me to the bone and I knew that it was time to dig out my long-john underwear. It wasn't just cool or chilly outside, it was bitter cold. The temperature at daylight was twenty-eight degrees, but of course in this country the thermometer tells you very little. I have experienced weather below zero that was really very pleasant, while twenty-eight degrees on the prairie can freeze a man to death. The difference lies in the presence or absence of wind. A thermometer isn't affected by wind, but the human body is, especially if it happens to be a-horseback.

Well, I could see that this wasn't going to be one of the better days I had chosen for a roundup. I got a cup of coffee and started thinking about what I should do. I didn't want to send a crew out into this kind of weather, but the cattle had to be worked sometime. I had gotten together a crew of nine. My wife had spent the previous day cooking and preparing the roundup meal. Everything was ready and I didn't want to call it off at the last minute. Around seven, I looked out the window and saw that it had started snowing, first little pellets of ice and then big flakes that were driven straight south by the stiff wind. Well, that was it. I would have to call off the roundup.

The phone rang. It was Virgil Dean in Beaver. "Kinda nasty outside, John," he said. "What do you think?"

I thought about it a moment. "Oh, come on out and we'll see what the weather does."

As soon as I hung up the phone, it rang again. This time it was Jim Gregg in Beaver. "Hi, Johnny, have you looked outside lately? There's something falling from the sky. I think it's snow. Are you going to try to work cattle today?"

I told him to come on out. He made some comment about my sanity and said he was on his way.

The phone rang again. This time it was Tom Ellzey. Driving up from the LZ Ranch in Texas, he had run into heavy snow around Elmwood, Oklahoma. He wondered if he should come on to the ranch or turn back. I told him to come on if he could, turn back if the snow got worse. Then I went to the closet and dug out my warmest clothes.

It had taken me several years to learn how to dress for the kind of severe cold we would face today. After freezing my tail off for two winters on the Crown Ranch, I had devoted a lot of time and thought to the best way of dressing to protect myself from that bone-chilling, wind-driven kind of cold. I am tall and thin and don't carry much flesh, so I am bothered by cold more than a lot of men who work outside.

The parts of me most affected by severe cold were my hands, feet, and neck. I had tried several types of insulated work gloves sold in local stores, but they hadn't helped much, so I invested twenty dollars in the best pair of ski gloves I could find in Dallas. They did the job, and I considered that one of the smartest investments I ever made. With my feet, I experimented with different boots, socks, and combinations of the two. The combination that worked the best for me was a pair of boots two sizes larger than I ordinarily wore, with one pair of thin nylon socks and one of heavy wool boot socks. I found that if I wore two pairs of wool socks instead of one, I lost some of the circulation in my feet and they stayed cold all the time.

Keeping the wind from blowing down my neck was another problem. I discovered that it was impossible to stay warm when my neck and throat were exposed. When I started wearing a cotton bandanna around my neck in the winter, I stopped catching colds. I later improved on the bandanna by having the lady in the local boot shop make me a collar of sheepskin that snapped tight around my neck and kept the wind from invading my body.

I dressed my upper body in layers: T-shirt, long-john underwear, flannel shirt, lined leather vest, and a lined bluejean jacket. The leather vest was especially important, since I found nothing that blunted the sting of wind better than leather. With the leather to stop the wind and the layers of cotton to provide insulation (cotton doesn't scratch the way wool does, and it doesn't give you a feeling of bulk), I was able to stay warm in the coldest weather. On my legs I wore long-johns, blue jeans, and leather chaps. Once again, the leather cut the wind and the cotton provided the insulation.

It took me fifteen or twenty minutes to put all these clothes on, but, once dressed, I was ready to face Mother Nature's wrath. I went down to the barn and saddled my horse, left him standing in the snow, and returned to the house to wait for the crew.

Jim Gregg arrived first. Jim stood six feet six inches tall, and with all his winter clothes on he looked like a grizzly bear. And he sounded like one too. He had come early so that he would have ample time to harass me for ordering this kind of weather for a branding day. Then Virgil and Terry Dean drove up. With them was John Hesler, the bank officer from Beaver who often rode on roundup crews when ranchers needed an extra hand. This was a bank holiday, and I guess Hesler had thought it would be nice to get out in the sunshine. He hadn't planned on riding in a blizzard, and Virgil claimed—I won't say it's the truth—Virgil claimed that when he went by to pick up Hesler, our cow-boy-banker was hiding under the covers and had to be dragged, kicking and screaming, out to the pickup.

Next to arrive were Mr. and Mrs. Arnold Good, who lived south of Perryton and often came up to the Crown Ranch to ride in my roundups. With them was their son Keith, trust officer at the Booker bank and my boss. The last to arrive was Tom Ellzey. He had almost turned back in the snowstorm, and he was already beginning to regret that he hadn't.

It was about eight o'clock by this time. We brewed another pot of coffee and sat around talking. At eight-thirty it was still snowing. By nine o'clock it was snowing harder than ever. No roundup today, we decided. Then around nine-thirty the snow stopped and the clouds began to break. Everyone waited for someone else to be the first to leave. No one left. At ten o'clock Virgil looked out the window and said, "Well, if we're going to do it, we'd better get started." I had lacked the courage to suggest this. With much grumbling and complaining, the crew pulled on chaps and coats and went out into the cold.

It was quite a shock, getting on a horse in that wind. We were fortunate that in rounding up the west pasture we were able to ride south for two miles, which meant that we had our backs to the wind. By the time we started the cattle north, we had adjusted to the cold and were receiving some warmth from our horses' bodies. Riding north against the wind, I could feel my face growing numb and my breath freezing in my beard, but I was never uncomfortably cold. All those layers did their job.

After gathering the west, we rounded up the middle and big east pastures and put each bunch into a separate trap. Then the hard part began. We had to pair up the calves with their mothers and cut them into the corral.

Any time you are working with pairs (that is, cows

The only barrier to the wind between the North Pole and the Crown Ranch.

with baby calves), shifting them around or moving them from one pasture to another, you must be very careful to keep mothers and babies together. If a calf is separated from its mother, several things can happen, all of them bad. Since the digestive system of a young calf has not developed to the point that it can digest grass and roughage, it must have milk to survive. If it is separated from its mother for several days, it will weaken and die. Or, at the very best, it may survive on a bit of grass and milk stolen from other cows. A calf steals milk by grabbing an udder and drinking a few swallows before the cow realizes that he's a thief and kicks him off. By spring, this orphan calf or dogie will be a runt, its growth stunted by poor nutrition. There is also the possibility that, in the process of bawling to find its mother, it will attract hungry coyotes. A mother cow can fight off a prowling coyote, or even several of them, but a baby calf is defenseless.

So, when you are shifting cows and calves from one pasture to another, you have to pair them up. You ride through the herd and wait for a calf to mother up. Since a cow will allow only her own calf to suck and will kick at a strange calf, a nursing calf is the most positive form of identification. When the calf takes hold of the udder, you ride into the herd, cut the pair off from the rest of the cattle, and drive them into the corral. You do it as quietly as possible, so as not to get the herd stirred up.

This can be pleasant work in the spring or on a nice warm day in the fall. But on November 11, 1976, on that bald hill in Beaver County, with the north wind whistling over our heads, it was not the least bit pleasant. John Hesler told me later that he had never been as cold in his entire life as he was that day, waiting for those calves to find their mommas.

Finally we got all the pairs cut off, turned out the dry cows, and began branding. By this time it was late afternoon. The sun was going down and so was the temperature. As I recall, we finished up around seven o'clock and we had to brand the last twenty calves by the lights of a pickup.

Well, it was a roundup that none of us would ever forget. For the next six months my cowboy friends heaped abuse on me in such quantities that I couldn't even make a witty response. Word of the North Pole Roundup spread, and it became a popular joke around Beaver that when the weather turned foul, Erickson was going to round up and brand. Or that if you wanted to ruin a string of pretty days, just have Erickson call up his crew and set a date for a branding.

After enduring this kind of abuse from the cowboys, I became a bit sensitive on the subject, and when the time came for the fall branding of 1977 I wanted to be certain that the weather would be tolerable. One North Pole Roundup had given us some good yarns to tell and embellish in our old age; two North Pole Roundups would be entirely too many.

For some reason, I waited until December to set the roundup date. I don't remember why, except that maybe I was waiting for more calves to hit the ground. The first week in December brought us pleasant weather: no snow or rain, no blustery northers, no severe cold. The mornings were chilly and damp, but by noon the temperature had climbed up into the fifties. I listened to the long-range forecast on the radio and learned that the weather wizards were predicting fair and mild. I set the date for December 8 and crossed my fingers.

Surely, I told myself, the odds were in my favor. Surely, I told myself, I couldn't posibly draw the black bean two years in a row. Surely.

The day before the roundup was beautiful—warm, calm, not a cloud in the hazy fall sky. When I retired for the night, there was not a breath of wind. When I awoke the following morning, I heard that sound again: moaning and whistling. The glass in the windows was vibrating. Outside, tumbleweeds loped across the yard and piled up on the north side of the fence. I experienced a feeling of *déjà vu*, a sense that I had been here before. I went to the closet and dug out my long-johns. The phone rang. It was Jim Gregg.

"Well, Johnny, you've done it again," he chirped. "How do you manage to do this year after year?"

"Shut up," I explained.

The crew arrived at eight: Mark Mayo, Sandy Hagar, and Ron Salaska, none of whom had attended the first North Pole Roundup, and Tom Ellzey, Jim Gregg, and Virgil and Terry Dean, all veterans from the year before. They greeted me at the door with leers, snarls, and smart remarks. Their fun was shot-lived. After downing one cup of coffee, we hit the saddles.

As I recall, we parted that morning thinking that this day wasn't going to be as cold as the first North Pole Roundup. By the time we had gathered the west pasture and had driven the cattle two miles into the north wind, that little illusion had evaporated. The temperature was dropping by the hour. This day would not only be as bad as the one in 1976, it would be worse. By noon the mercury had dropped to twenty-three degrees, and I would guess that the wind chill factor was somewhere around fifteen or twenty below zero.

There is a point at which it is just too cold to work cattle. When we stopped for lunch, after gathering two pastures and sorting off the pairs, I had decided that I couldn't ask these men, most of whom had once considered themselves my friends, to endure the cold any longer. I announced that after lunch we would turn the cattle out to pasture and finish up the branding on a better day. There were no objections.

Up at the house, Kris had a big pot of hot chocolate on the stove, and that helped to thaw out our gizzards. After we had put away a good hot roundup meal, we found pillows and sprawled on the floor. The heat must have gone to our heads, because someone—I don't even remember who the fool was—said, "We've got the cattle up. Why don't we just go ahead and work them." The others agreed. We pulled on all our clothes, left the cozy warmth of the house, and, moving like robots in all our layers of clothing, plodded down to the corral, where we had sixty-six calves waiting to be branded and worked.

As I said, there is a point at which it is too cold to work cattle. We were right at that point, and maybe even a little on the other side. Shortly after we began, we discovered that our equipment was beginning to malfunction. Vaccine was freezing in the vaccine gun and we had to hold it over the branding fire to thaw it out. The disinfectant we used to sterilize the castrating knife and dehorning equipment began to freeze. Blood from the dehorning wounds froze on our gloves, leggings, faces, wherever it landed. The propane we used to heat the branding fire began to freeze up and we couldn't keep the irons hot. To keep the fire going, we had to hold the propane bottle over the flames. Tom Ellzey, who was cutting the bull calves and couldn't wear gloves, probably suffered the most from the cold. Blood froze on his bare hands, and he had to wipe them on a rag and stop from time to time to warm them over the branding fire.

By the time we had worked the calves and turned everything back into the pastures, we had established an all-time record for a miserable roundup. The first North Pole Roundup had been bad, but the second had surpassed it. Today, there are eight men in the Texas and Oklahoma panhandles who will never forget that day. But worst of all, they will never let me foget it. When we are seventy-five years old, too worn out and broke down to do anything but chew and whittle, they will still be talking about December 8, 1977. And I suppose Tom Ellzey will still be saying, "Well, there's one thing about Erickson's roundups. They were never dull."

WILD CATTLE

12
WILD CATTLE

Thus far, we have seen the Crown Ranch cattle at their best, simply because on roundup days I had enough crew around to manhandle them. They were at their worst when I rode out to face them alone—which was most of the time.

This ranch was a one-man operation, and I was the only employee. Most of the time I had to depend on my own wits and skill, such as they were, to get the job done. I was being paid to operate the ranch, and I tried not to inflict my problems on my neighbors unless it was necessary.

It took me about a year and a half to adjust to this herd of cattle, to learn their habits, and to comprehend the nature of my job among them. What I learned—and found very difficult to accept—was that they were virtually unmanageable; that any time I set out to accomplish a task, the odds were at least fifty-fifty that I would fail; and that there was no such thing as a simple job.

On an ordinary ranch with ordinary cattle, you rate some jobs as difficult and you know in advance that the

Coming in with a small bunch of heifers. On an ordinary ranch with gentle cattle, two cowboys could have done this job easily. Erickson used five riders and needed every one of them before the heifers gave up. Erickson, mounted on Suds, is riding the point position and is looking back to see if the cattle are going to make a run.

odds against your accomplishing them are high. For example, if one man goes out into the pasture and tries to move twenty-five cows into another pasture, he knows that he might not get the job done, or that he might enjoy only partial success. But if he goes out to cut out and bring in one animal, he has every reason to suppose that he can do it. That was not the case in my position. Moving twenty-five head of cows by myself was out of the question; it couldn't be done. And bringing one cow to the house was a chancy affair. Sometimes I could do it and sometimes I couldn't. I would guess that I succeeded about sixty percent of the time.

I once made this statement to a friend who was a good cowboy and a much better roper than I. He snorted at the very idea that one man couldn't bring one cow to the house a hundred percent of the time. His answer to a wild cow was a nylon rope. If she defied him, he would rope her, throw a trip on her, bust her a few times, and then either drive or drag her into the pens. Now, I don't pretend to be the best cowboy in the country. I have met a few cowboys who probably could have roped, busted, and dragged every cow on the ranch and eventually taught them some manners. But I was never that keen on roping cows.

I was an average roper riding average horses, and the prospect of roping, busting, and dragging full-grown cows, which weighed anywhere from nine hundred to thirteen hundred pounds, did not appeal to me. I did it when I had to, but I certainly didn't go looking for opportunities. I think perhaps roping wild cows is fun only when you're working with other cowboys. Two or more good hands can tie on to just about anything and come out of it in good shape. If you rope the head, one of your buddies can always pick up the heels, stretch the cow out, and hold her while you get your rope back. If she wants to attack your horse once you've got her on the string, another cowboy

can rope her head, and with two of you pulling her in opposite directions, she won't be able to hurt anyone.

But most of the time I was out in the pasture by myself. I could have roped a wild cow, but once I had her
roped, then what would I have done with her? That was
the question that always came to my mind. I didn't have
anyone to back me up, no one to help me get my rope off
the cow's head, no one to come to my rescue if she tried to
put a horn through my horse's rib cage, and no one to help
me drag her through a mile of sandhills. I was also keenly
aware of the fact that if I got hurt out in the pasture, no one
would even suspect anything was wrong for several hours,
and by the time someone found me, I could have lain out
there for half a day or more with some hideous injury.

The lariat rope is a very useful piece of equipment,
and I admire any man who knows how to use it. There are
times when you have to use it, but there are also times
when you are better off leaving it alone. I think it would
have been a little foolish of me to have spent my time busting cows out in the pasture, all three hundred of them, on
the pretense that I was "teaching them a lesson." If cows are
wild to start with, I doubt that you can improve them by
chasing and roping them.

Once wildness has gotten into a herd of cattle, there is
no simple way of getting it out. Well, there is one simple
way: sell every damned one of them and start all over with
heifers. But other than that, there is no simple solution.
Wild old cows teach the young cows, and mommas teach
their babies. Perhaps a good stout dose of Valium in the feed
would have improved them, but I never got around to trying
that.

The worst part of working with wild cattle is that
every job, no matter how small or routine, becomes an ordeal. In the winter of 1975, I noticed that a big Charolais-
cross cow had lost her calf, and it appeared to me that the

calf had died because the cow wasn't producing enough milk. That is the kind of cow you don't want to keep around, because she will probably starve her calf again next year, and you had better put wheels under her while she's still fresh on your mind.

So I rode out into the pasture to cut her out and take her to the home pens. I walked my horse so as not to frighten her. As soon as she saw me, at a distance of three hundred yards, she curled her tail and headed south in a run. Along the way she picked up ten or twelve more cows, who fell in right behind her. Just to keep her in sight I had to kick my horse into a high lope. I waited for them to slow down or stop, but they kept right on going. I followed them for a mile and finally decided it was time to make my move. I galloped into the middle of them, cut the cow off from the bunch, and turned her north toward the pens.

She was still running, even though her tongue was hanging out and she was slobbering. She ran until she couldn't run another step, then, weaving back and forth, she stopped in a sand draw, turned to face me, and prepared to fight. I popped her on the nose with my rope, but it didn't do any good. Every time I rode in close enough to pop her, she came after me.

I left the blankety-blank there and rode home with the bitter taste of defeat in my mouth. But I was determined to get her off the ranch one way or another, and I changed my tactics. The following day I spotted her in a bunch of cows that were grazing on the north end of the pasture. Slowly and patiently I managed to call them into the pens, using feed as the lure. Once I had gotten them into the corral, I cut her into a pen by herself and turned the rest back into the pasture.

That was Monday. The livestock auction in Beaver was held on Wednesday. All I had to do was give her feed and water for two days, load her into the trailer Wednesday morning, and haul her to the sale.

But it wasn't that simple. Once she found herself alone in the pen, she went berserk. When I approached her (on the other side of the fence), she began circling the pen. She smashed into an iron gate, bloodying her nose and bending the gate. She tried to go over the top of a fence made of steel landing mats and cable, and once again she left her impression on the steel. Snorting bubbles of blood, she turned toward me and charged. Had there not been a five-foot steel fence between us, she would have eaten me for lunch.

What had I done to provoke her? I had approached her with a bucket of oats and a flake of alfalfa hay.

Next problem: How do you load this kind of animal into a stock trailer? Under ordinary circumstances, you walk into the pen, shoo the cow into the alley, and persuade her with a stick to jump into the trailer. I didn't even consider stepping into the pen with this lunatic cow. Since she began snorting and pawing the ground when I was still fifty feet away from the gate, I had a fair idea what she would do if I put myself within her range. So, with my natural aversion to being mauled, I decided to use cunning.

Clearly it was going to take some time to load this cow. It might take hours or even days. I wanted her off the ranch, and I didn't intend to miss getting her into the Beaver sale. I decided to start at once trying to load her, and once I got her loaded, to leave her in the trailer until I was ready to haul her to the sale on Wednesday morning.

I backed the stock trailer up to the alley, opened the back gate, and placed hay and water inside. Then I tied a lariat rope to the trailer gate and ran the other end to a post, where I could pull the rope and close the gate without standing in the alley where she could run over me. I un-hooked the trailer from the pickup, set the corral gates so that the cow could get into the alley, and went on about my business. Several times that day I checked my trap. The cow never did go into the trailer. When she saw me, she perked up her ears, snorted, lowered her head, and began running up and down the alley. I didn't dare go any closer, since I had every reason to suppose that if she really wanted to, she could flatten any fence on the ranch, including the five-foot landing mat fence that was holding her. It is astounding the amount of damage a twelve-hundred-pound animal can do once she has set her mind to it.

Tuesday morning I sneaked down to the barn and peeked around a corner to see where she was. Aha! Hunger had finally gotten the best of her. She had gone into the trailer and was eating the alfalfa. If I could close the trailer gate, I would have her captured. I knew that if she saw me she would come out of the trailer like a freight train, so I walked out into the horse pasture, got down in a draw where she couldn't see me, and followed it around to the south. There, I entered the corral at the bottom end and proceeded to crawl on hands and knees toward my lariat rope, just as though I were stalking a wild animal. By the time she saw me, it was already too late for her. I yanked the rope and the gate swung shut with a slam. Had she hit the gate at that point, before I had secured it with the latch, she would have escaped and I might never have trapped her again. But she didn't test it. I latched it, and just to be sure, I tied it shut with a short piece of chain.

I left her in the trailer the rest of the day and that night. Ordinarily, when you take an animal to the sale, you keep plenty of feed and water in front of it so it won't lose weight. Since livestock sells by the pound, lost weight, or "shrink," is lost money. But by this time I really didn't care what the cow looked like when I delivered her to the sale. All I wanted to do was get her off the ranch without getting myself hurt or tearing up the trailer in the process. I didn't go near the trailer.

The next morning I hooked on to the trailer and off we went to Beaver to the sale. This livestock auction consisted of a sand-filled ring surrounded by a stout fence made of welded pipe. The auctioneer occupied a high platform at one end of the ring where he could see the cattle and also the buyers, who sat in bleachers on the other side of the fence. The cattle entered the ring through one gate and left through another which opened into the scale pen. There every animal was weighed. Two or three men worked in the ring, operating the gates, stirring the cattle around so that buyers could study them for lameness and other defects, and helping the auctioneer spot bidders in the crowd. (Cattle buyers are notoriously coy about placing their bids. Some will lift a finger, some will give a slight nod of the head, and others will do no more than move their lips.)

I was in the audience that afternoon and watched my crossbred cow go through the ring. I wouldn't have missed that show for anything. Before they opened the gate, someone back in the yards yelled, "Watch her, boys!" The gate swung open, and in she came like a charging buffalo. The ring boys saw her coming and dived for the fence. I was right proud of the old hussy. She cleared the ring in one swath, and then, once she had sold, the boys had a hard time getting her out of the ring and onto the scales. Every time one of them came off the fence and popped at her with a whip, she attacked him. Though I wished no hard luck on the boys working the ring that day, I watched this exhibition with a feeling of tremendous satisfaction. It had taken me four days to gather, load, and deliver this unutterable wretch to the sale barn, a job which should have taken no more than an hour, and it made my wicked heart sing to see her causing misery to someone else.

One of the small rewards of handling wild cattle lies in the fact that, once you get them to the sale barn, you can go to sleep that night knowing that in just a few days they will be made up into hot dogs. A hot dog roasting over an open fire is close enough to the old Protestant vision of hellfire and damnation to give you the feeling that there is justice in the universe.

In October 1974 the trust department of the bank decided to go into a crossbreeding program in which we would run Red Brangus bulls on our herd of mostly Hereford cows. Keith Good and I made a trip down to the Oasis Ranch east of Canadian, Texas, and looked at Bill McQuiddy's herd of Red Brangus cows. He had some two- and three-year-old bulls for sale, and we decided to buy eight of them. On Halloween eve I hauled them to the Crown Ranch. From then on, I referred to them as the Halloween bulls. The name seemed appropriate, since they had a creaturely, rather evil look about them, which I attributed to the three-eighths Brahman blood that ran in their veins.

I had never worked much around Brahman or part-Brahman cattle, and I didn't know their habits and mannerisms. I could look at a Hereford bull and tell what was on his mind. If he was snuffy and wanted to fight, he would show it. But these Brangus bulls were another matter. Either they didn't show their thoughts as openly as a Hereford or else I wasn't able to recognize the signals. To me, they appeared sullen and waspy, yet they were very gentle and easy to handle. I kept them in the corral for several days and walked among them without incident. They were more inclined to kick than a Hereford bull, but you expect that in any animal with Angus breeding. (For some reason, Angus cattle are notorious kickers.) After keeping the Halloween bulls in the pens for several days, I loaded them into the trailer and distributed them over the ranch.

In November Keith asked me to haul the bulls to Beaver and get them semen tested, to be sure that they were fertile. This is a common precaution a buyer takes in purchasing bulls, and we had merely forgotten to do it. So I rode out into the west pasture, gathered up four of the bulls, and drove them to the pens. I backed the trailer up to the alley and began what I thought would be the routine task of loading them. I had loaded these same bulls only two weeks before and had not experienced the slightest difficulty, and I expected none this time.

I was in for a surprise. I walked into the pen, expecting to push them into the alley, whence they would hop into the trailer like pups. I was caught completely unprepared when one of the larger bulls suddenly whirled and came after me. I raced him to the nearest gate and bailed over the top.

If a bull never shows aggressive tendencies, you tend to think that he never will. But once he tries to get into your pocket, you find yourself thinking that he'll try it every time. The job which, only minutes before, I had considered routine and simple now took on a new and sinister dimension. It was complicated by my difficulty in getting any emotional reading on the faces of these Halloween bulls. The bull that had come after me had showed no signs of irritation. One minute he had been trotting toward the trailer, and an instant later he had turned on me. What had produced this change? I didn't know.

Well, I had a fine mess on my hands. I had orders to get the bulls tested, and somehow I had to load them into the trailer—ideally without getting myself smashed and battered. I stepped back into the pen with the four bulls, but this time I stayed close to the fence, just in case I was forced into another hasty retreat. It appeared to me that the two smaller bulls were not inclined to fight, so I cut them off and followed them down the alley. They hopped right into the trailer and I shut the middle gate behind them, securing them in the front compartment. I hoped that with two animals already in the trailer, the remaining two would load easier. It often works that way with herd animals. And sometimes it doesn't.

I returned to the pen to start the other two bulls into the alley. They were standing in the far corner, watching me with their heads up and their big floppy ears pointed forward. Each bull was a thousand pounds of pure muscle wrapped in a dark red skin. I didn't care to get too close to them, so I started throwing rocks to make them move. They sniffed the corner of the pen, looking for a hole, then went charging around the fence, through the gate, and into the alley. They moved so fast I had to run behind them in order to be in position to shut the gate if and when they jumped into the trailer.

There is a trick to shutting that trailer gate. You want to shut it immediately behind the animal, while he is still facing forward. Otherwise, if he is wild or nervous, he may turn and try to break out before you have latched the gate. If you are standing behind the gate when he hits it, the collision can produce some unwanted side effects. As they say in this country, it's hard on clothes.

With this in mind, I sprinted behind the bulls. I had to get closer to them than I really wanted to, otherwise I had no chance to shut the gate when they loaded into the trailer. This maneuver soon degenerated into something approaching comedy. One instant I was sprinting to catch up with the bulls, chasing them down the alley. At the trailer gate, they sniffed the ground, swapped ends, and came straight toward me. All at once they were chasing me. I swapped ends, ran, and climbed the fence. The bulls went back into the pen and waited for me to make my next move.

My next move was to call for help. These bulls made me uneasy. You can say all you want to about the nice disposition of Brahman and Brahman-cross cattle, but I will always maintain that they are a different breed of cat. Cattle with Brahman blood just don't behave like British cattle, and the difference in temperament falls on the negative side of the ledger. I think Brahman-type animals are quicker, more athletic, and more prone to fight in a tight spot. It was the quickness of these bulls that impressed me most. As the saying goes, they could turn on a dime and give you a nickle's change. Working with them in close quarters, you had to stay alert all the time, and even so your reaction time was likely to be a split second too slow. With bulls, that split second can be important.

I felt that, working alone, I had gone about as far as I dared. The bulls were getting hot and snuffy, and the more I choused them now the more chance there was that I would end up on the short end of an argument. I went to the house and called Sandy Hagar.

Sandy was in his early sixties at this time and had worked around animals all his life. In his prime, he had been—this is his own description, not mine—a "big lard-tailed kid" who, at 210 pounds, had used muscle to solve problems. But over the years he had been run over and thumped around enough that he had learned to use his head. He could always figure out the easiest way of doing a job.

When he arrived, he got right down to important business: he rolled a Prince Albert cigarette. How he was able to perform that delicate task with such aplomb, I never understood, for his hands were as big as skillets. Yet he could whip up a "hot tamale" in about sixty seconds, and, in a pinch, had been known to do it with one hand. He rolled one for himself and then rolled one for me. I was an abysmal failure at rolling smokes. When Sandy rolled me a P.A., he would never lick the paper at the top, to spare me from cold germs and such. He would hand it to me and say, "There, hammerhead, lap the top."

We lit up, hunkered down, and talked about my problem. I gave him my opinion of the bulls. We studied the pens and came up with a plan. Sandy would stand behind the trailer gate, out of sight. When I brought the bulls up the alley, I would try to push them into the trailer with a heavy wooden crowding gate, and when they jumped inside, Sandy would close the trailer gate behind them. We rigged up the trailer gate with a rope, so that he could close it by pulling the rope. That way, if the bulls whirled and came back, neither of us would be in the gate's path when it flew open.

When everything was ready, Sandy took his place and I went into the pen to bring the bulls. I pelted them with rocks and sticks and horse biscuits and started them moving. When they moved out, it was at a lope. They ran out the gate and into the alley toward the trailer, and I fell in behind them, yelling and waving a piece of windmill rod. When they reached the trailer, one of the bulls whirled and came back at me. I moved to the side, and he thundered right over my tracks. The other bull had stepped up into the trailer with his front feet. Sandy pulled the rope and put pressure on him. The bull didn't move. He stood there, half in and half out, sniffing the air. I made a quick assessment of the situation and decided to swing the wooden crowding gate behind him. I figured that once he felt the pressure of that heavy gate on his rump, he would hop into the trailer.

I think, had we been loading Hereford bulls, it would have worked, but with the Red Brangus, it didn't. When he felt the gate behind him, he snorted, whirled, and, using his amazing quickness and acceleration, hit the crowding gate with a full head of steam. As I saw what was about to happen, my mind moved quickly, but my body reactions were a bit too slow. I knew the bull was going to hit the gate. I knew the gate was not latched to the post and that there was nothing behind it but my body. I knew that I weighed 170 pounds, and that the bull weighed half a ton. I knew exactly what would happen. A calm voice inside my head said, "John, old pal, if you put your weight against that gate when he hits it, he's going to knock you into next week. It might be a good idea for you to drop that gate and run." But my body followed instinct. When the bull whirled around, I leaned into the gate with all my strength, in effect betting my body and health that the gate would bluff him out and turn him back into the trailer. It wasn't a stupid decision. It just happened to be wrong. Most cattle can be stopped with a gate, even if it isn't latched. Most cattle can be bluffed out. Most cattle won't try to run through a heavy gate if they can see it. This bull wasn't most cattle.

When he hit the gate, he had his thousand pounds in high gear. He didn't even break stride. It was like an explosion. In a tangle of arms and legs, I flew through the air and smashed into a fence made of steel landing mats. The distance I traveled in that split second was the arc described by the gate, from closed to open position. I measured it the following day with a tape. It came to eleven feet. I don't think my feet ever touched the ground through that whole distance. That will give some indication of the brute strength of the bull—which, by the way, was only a bit more than half-grown.

I hit the steel fence with my head, and with such force that I could hear my skin and bones squish and groan. Later, when the shock began to wear off, I discovered that I had made contact with the fence in four other places: both elbows, my left shoulder, and my right shin. But at the moment of impact, my main concern was my head. I thought I was hurt, and I expected to see blood. I got to my hands and knees and crawled around in the dirt, waiting for the damage reports to come in from the various parts of my body.

I thought Sandy's reaction to the incident was odd. He laughed. Even as he asked if I was hurt, he was laughing. It irked me just a little bit, since at that moment I could hardly speak and was still not sure of the extent of my injuries. His laughter seemed in poor taste.

Since then I have noticed the same reaction among rodeo cowboys. I once saw a young bull rider get thrown completely over a hogwire fence. He missed hitting a light pole with his head by a matter of inches. His friends, who were watching from the bucking chutes, reacted with uproarious laughter. So, while laughter may seem an inappropriate response to physical danger, especially to the party most intimately involved, it is apparently a natural human response and one that does not reflect malice, meanness, or lack of feeling.

There is another explanation for Sandy's reaction, and this one doesn't require any psychology: I may have looked very funny flying through the air.

Well, I came out of the wreck with nothing more than lumps, bruises, and ruffled feelings. Sandy and I turned all four bulls back into the pasture. I never did haul them to town, and I never again tried to load one of them into a stock trailer.

I have attributed the temperament of these bulls to their Brangusness, to the three-eighths Brahman blood in their breeding. I should say, however, that when we received the Halloween bulls on the Oasis Ranch, we had no trouble handling or loading them. After I had kept them up in the pens for three days, I had no trouble loading them. But after they had run in the pasture on the Crown Ranch for two weeks, they became very difficult to handle.

What had brought about this change in only two weeks? I don't know the answer, but I can't help wondering to what extent it was a reflection of the ranch and its herd of wild cattle. You could say that it could have happened anywhere. But, as in the case of the Broken Leg Roundup, it didn't happen anywhere, it happened on the Crown ranch. At some point, what you first regard as coincidence begins to fit a pattern: every little job becomes an ordeal; nothing is easy.

She doesn't look wild, but that's because she just delivered her first calf and now she's relaxing in the warm sunshine. Before he took this picture, Bill Ellzey had to assist in the delivery.

13
A BITTER LESSON

During my first months on the Crown Ranch, I learned that it was very difficult for one man on horseback to perform the chores that are routine on most ranches. I learned to roll with the punches. When I had a job I didn't think I could do alone, I waited until I had some help.

Toward the end of April I had a long list of pasture jobs that needed attention, so I called Bill Ellzey and asked if I could hire him for a few days' work. He said yes, and on the afternoon of April 27 he arrived in his mud-spattered blue Chevrolet, pulling Suds in a dilapidated old two-wheel horse trailer. It was late in the day, but I wanted to get a few jobs out of the way before dark. We loaded Suds and Dollarbill into my stock trailer and drove over to the east end of the ranch.

A neighbor's steer had gotten into the big east pasture about a month before. I had put him out of the pasture once and he had come back. I had tried to eject him a second time, but he had fallen in with a bunch of wild cows, and

after a merry chase around the pasture I had decided to
wait until I had some help. He weighed around six hundred
pounds, and I had not wanted to try to rope him and drag
him into the trailer by myself. My trailer was covered with
a metal roof from front to back, and it was difficult for one
man to drag an animal into it by himself. It could be done,
but it required the use of two ropes, a stout horse, and some
good luck. Had the trailer been only partially covered,
without a roof over the back compartment, the job would
have been fairly simple.

We found the steer on the north end of the pasture,
grazing with five or six cows near the gate we wanted to put
him through. If we could cut him away from the cows,
putting him out would be simple. We opened the gate and
unloaded our horses. As soon as the cows saw the horses,
they threw their heads up, curled their tails over their
backs, and headed west at a run. We fell in behind them,
closing in from opposite sides, and cut the steer off from
the bunch. On the north end we tried to put him through
the gate, but by then he had decided that he wanted to go
south. We tried to turn him but he wouldn't turn. As a last
resort, we took down our ropes.

I took the first shot and missed. Bill moved in, made a
good shot, but couldn't fish it around the steer's neck. I
loaded up again and caught him by the horns. While I held
him, Bill went for the pickup and trailer. We dragged him
into the trailer and hauled him to his home pasture. Then
we loaded our horses again and drove to the little east
pasture. I had some two-year-old heifers in the little east,
and since there was one that was getting heavy with calf, I
wanted to cut her out and take her to the house where I
could watch her more closely and assist her if she had
trouble delivering her first calf.

We scouted the heifers from the pickup before we
unloaded our horses. We spotted the one we wanted, and I

made the moronic statement that we should try to take her
slow and easy.

   We unloaded the horses, the heifers bolted and ran, we
hit the saddles, and off we went in pursuit. Since cow
brutes sometimes drive better in pairs than they do alone,
we cut off the heavy heifer and took another with her and
pointed them west toward the middle pens. They ran every
step of the way until they reached the corral gate, which we
had already opened. There they stopped. As we rode up to
them, we could see that we had a pair of lunatics on our
hands. Panting, ears perked, sniffing the ground, they
looked in every direction for a place to run—every
direction except toward the pens. All they had to do was
take five steps to the west and we would be finished with
them. But they weren't looking at the gate.

   Bill and I knew the conventional response to this type
of situation: you sit quietly on your horse and hold the
cattle in front of the gate. Sooner or later, after they have
milled and squirmed and sniffed for a while, they will see
the gate and go through it. We waited five minutes. The
heifers still had not gone into the pen. I said, "All right,
that didn't work. Let's see if we can push them in." We
rode toward them. When they made a move in the wrong
direction, we cut them off. Finally the larger of the two
threw up her head and ran into the pens. The other
followed.

   We sighed with relief. That wasn't so bad. The sun
had dropped over the horizon and it would be dark in
another thirty minutes. We had penned the cattle just in
time. I fastened the gate with a piece of light chain and we
started riding back to the pickup. We had accomplished our
job, and we were feeling pretty good about it.

   With our backs turned, we didn't notice what the
heifers were doing. They ran around the pen several times,
sniffing every corner and looking for an escape hole. Then,

with the big one in the lead, they galloped around the pen one last time, piled into the gate, and broke the chain. The gate flew open, and we had two heifers that appeared to be heading for South Texas. I won't repeat what I said. I dug my spurs into Dollarbill's sides and off we went over the sandhills and through the sagebrush.

The heifers ran south down the fence. I didn't want to crowd them, for fear they would go through the fence into the middle pasture, so I got out in front so that I would be in a position to hold them when they came to the corner. I figured we could hold them in the corner for a few minutes, give them time to settle down, and then start them back toward the pens. If that didn't work, we would rope the big one and drag her in.

That was a sensible plan, and it should have worked. But when the heifers reached the corner, they didn't even slow down. The big one was in the lead. When she saw her path blocked up ahead, she crashed into the fence to her right. It so happened that there were some steel posts in the fence at that point, and I observed something that I had never seen before. Her front legs hit the fence with such force that sparks flew from the steel post, and it happened again when her back legs went over. Off she went in the middle pasture, with her head up in the air. A moment later the smaller heifer piled into the fence and joined her.

I rode over to where Bill was waiting. He flashed a sardonic smile. "Nice cattle."

"Yeah."

"Now what?"

I sighed. "Let's give them the night to settle down. We'll try again tomorrow."

We rode back to the trailer, grinding our teeth in silent rage. Our day had ended on a sour note of failure. We had been deprived of a feeling of accomplishment. Little did we know that the worst was yet to come.

The next morning we were in the saddle at eight-thirty

and spent four hours sorting off cow-calf pairs and moving them out of the west pasture. For some odd reason the work went smoothly and we didn't have any problems. We drove the cattle into a corner of the pasture, and I sorted off the pairs while Bill held herd.

After lunch, we were ready to go after the heifers. My wife wanted to ride with us, so I saddled Dollarbill for her and I rode Reno, the toughest horse on the ranch. As we rode toward the spot where we had last seen the heifers, we discussed our strategy. We would try to gather them quietly. If they wanted to go north, we would pen them in the middle pens. If they wanted to go west, we would take them all the way to the home corrals. If necessary and as a last resort, we would rope the big heifer.

We spotted them along the south fence, not far from the point where we had left them the night before. Some of Mark Mayo's cows were grazing on the other side of the fence. Our first objective would be to push the heifers away from the fence. They had proven the previous day that they were fence busters and we wanted to keep them away from the fence line. We spread out and closed in. We walked our horses and didn't make a sound. There is no way we could have approached them more peacefully. When the big heifer saw us, she threw up her head and bolted off to the northwest and we fell in behind her, putting ourselves between her and the fence. But after she had gone twenty-five yards, she reversed her direction and began running straight toward us. That told us something about the heifer. Any cow brute that runs toward a horse is crazy. I could see, just from the way she moved and carried her head, that we wouldn't be able to turn her or get a rope on her before she reached the fence, so I galloped away from her and told Bill and Kris to do the same. We backed off and waited to see what she would do, hoping that she would stop at the fence and give us another chance.

She plowed right into the fence, popped the staples

out of five posts, and kept right on going. The second heifer, brainless dupe that she was, followed and popped out a few more staples.

I rode over to talk with Bill. He thought we should just leave the heifers alone and call it quits. They were in Mark's pasture, but they weren't hurting anything. I know now that he was right, and had this incident occurred a year later, I would have left them alone. But I was mad and frustrated, and penning those heifers had become a matter of pride. I was the manager of this ranch, and dammit, I intended to manage it, whether those heifers liked it or not.

Bill had not been defeated by these cattle as often as I and didn't understand my feelings. He grumbled that I was making a stupid decision. I replied that he could do whatever he wanted to, but I was going after the heifers. I rode to the nearest gate and started south after the outlaws.

That was a big mistake.

I thought it would be a fairly easy job, but as I rode after them, I could see that the conditions were changing fast. The heifers were running south as hard as they could go. By the time I caught up with them, they were half a mile into Mark's pasture and showing no signs of wanting to stop or go back north. And worse, they were stirring up the whole pasture. Mark's cows had started running in bunches by themselves. The pasture resembled an anthill, with cattle running in all directions. I hoped that Mark was taking a nap or reading a book and wouldn't discover the circus we had brought to his ranch. By this time I no longer cared whether we penned the heifers or not. I just wanted to get them away from Mark's cattle before their wildness rubbed off.

I had to push old Reno to catch up with them. The big heifer was out in the lead, and trailing behind her were the smaller heifer and five or six YL cows. I got out in front of them and headed them west. About a mile away there was a pasture gate that opened into our west pasture. I decided to take them there. Bill had caught up with me by this time. I told him we would take them west and cut off Mark's cows as we went. He nodded that he understood the plan, but also communicated with his facial expression what he thought about it. Dumb.

As the west fence came into view, we cut off the last of Mark's cows and were down to our two heifers again. They didn't stop running until they reached the fence. I would have been delighted if they had gone through this fence, since it would have put them back on the Crown Ranch. But of course they didn't. I held them while Bill opened the gate, then I pushed them up the fence. If we could just get them through the gate, I was ready to quit.

They walked right past the gate. Bill stopped them, turned them around, and headed them back toward the gate. They went past it again. We repeated the maneuver, and still they wouldn't go through the gate. It was incredible. We were tired, they were tired, the horses were tired. We all wanted to quit and go home. All those heifers had to do was move four steps to the west and we would be through with them. But they seemed possessed of a demonic power that would not allow them to do the right thing.

Kris came riding up on Dollarbill and the three of us held the heifers in front of the gate. Surely they would see it in a minute. They were panting for breath. Their tongues were hanging out. Yet, after they had stood in the gate for five or ten minutes, they began to mill and look to the east. We had just brought them from the east. Why would they want to go back in that direction? We held them as long as we could, and then the big one broke away.

"All right," I yelled at Bill, "let's rope them and drag them out the gate." I fell in behind the big one, and Bill got after the little one.

If I had been able to catch my heifer on the first loop, this plan would have worked, but my rope seemed to have fallen under the same evil spell that had plagued us all afternoon. The heifer was tired and was running with her head down. I couldn't get a decent shot. My loop wouldn't fall over her head. It turned to the right. It turned to the left. It closed up. It glanced off her ear. By the time I finally caught her, I couldn't see the gate or Bill or Kris. The heifer was so tired she wouldn't drive. In the best tradition of Crown-branded cattle, she wanted to fight. I tried to drag her, but Reno was out of gas. So I sat there and waited for Bill to come. I figured we could heel her, stretch her out, tie her down, and go back to the house for the stock trailer.

I waited and waited. No sign of Bill. Kris came riding up. We were wondering what had become of Bill when I heard something. I looked toward the sound and saw Bill's heifer approaching—dragging his catch rope. She trotted right past us and kept on going. I told Kris to ride back to the gate and see what had happened to Bill. If she didn't find him, she should ride back to the house and bring the pickup and trailer so we could load my heifer. She left, and I was alone again with an angry heifer on my string. I kept looking off to the north, searching for a sign of Bill. I was worried that he might have gotten into a storm. I knew that Suds would buck if he ever got a rope under his tail. I was afraid that Bill might be hurt.

About ten minutes later he came riding over a hill from the east—very slowly. Geeze, I was glad to see him.

He looked at my heifer, looked at me, and snarled, "What are you gonna do now, *cowboy?*"

Bill and I had ridden many miles together, had been in some tight spots, and had exchanged a few harsh words, but we had never come as close to bloodshed as we were at that moment. Right then, I understood why cowboys quit carrying six-shooters.

There was a long silence. I swallowed my anger and asked how his heifer had gotten away with his rope, and he told me. He had been chasing the heifer and was about to rope her when she stopped and charged his horse. Suds moved out of her path and she passed them on the right side. On impulse, Bill pitched the loop over his shoulder and was not even looking at her when the rope closed around her neck. Off she went, and the rope started burning through his hand. Before he could dally to the horn, she had taken it away from him and was on a romp through the pasture.

In the years since this event occurred, Bill has taken a lot of ribbing about his famous over-the-shoulder shot, and I suppose people who have heard the story have wondered why he did such a thing. I know why he did it. It was a blind response to unbearable frustration, a feeling that can be understood only by cowboys who have been beaten and humiliated by cattle. I once heard the story of a cowboy who, after missing loop after loop, threw his rope into a stock tank and rode off. Another cowboy in the same state of rage bailed off his horse, pulled out his pocket knife, and cut his rope into four or five pieces. Given the circumstances, Bill's response was perfectly rational.

So there we were. We had one heifer dragging a rope through the pasture and another on the ground. Bill asked what I intended to do with mine. I said, well, let's tie her down with a pigging string and go get the other one. To which he replied, "Fine. I'll sit on your horse and *you* can tie her down." I think he was still mad.

He got off Suds and climbed into my saddle. I took my pigging string out of the saddlebag and walked down the rope toward the heifer. She was lying on her side and was so tired that I thought I could tie her down, even though she weighed seven hundred pounds. I caught her front leg and was reaching for a hind leg when she began to struggle. I held on as long as I could, then she overpowered me and I had to let go. She jumped to her feet and hit the end of the rope.

I had forgotten to mention to Bill that the rope was only dallied (wrapped) around the horn. He thought I had thrown two half-hitches over the horn and was tied solid, so he was not holding the rope when the heifer took out the slack. The rope spun around the horn three times, and zing, we had another heifer loose in the pasture. She headed east, dragging my rope behind her.

Bill slumped forward in the saddle and bowed his head. I swallowed a sudden impulse to scream and weep. It had started out to be such a simple job. All we had wanted to do was take one heifer to the house.

By this time Bill and I had broken off all communication. I hated his guts for turning the heifers loose—and for being right that we should have left them alone—and he hated mine for getting him into this incredible mess. We cinched up our poor dripping horses and loped over the hill to see if we could get our ropes back.

Quit? There was no chance of quitting now. We had two wild heifers running through the neighbor's pasture, each dragging a rope that hissed through the grass and frightened every cow brute within a quarter mile. But even worse, I was afraid that someone driving down the county road, which ran through the center of the pasture, would see the mess we had gotten ourselves into—or assume that someone had had a roping accident and call the sheriff. I hoped with all my heart that we could get our ropes back, get out of Mark's pasture, and sneak home without being observed.

We spotted my heifer in the southeast corner of the pasture and rode to her. She was so hot and snaky that she was ready to fight anything that approached her. This made it hard to get the rope off her neck, so we decided to drive her north and put her back into the middle pasture. At least then she would be away from Mark's cattle. So we started her north. Now and then she stopped and charged our horses. After she had made several razoos at Reno, I turned his hind end toward her, hoping he would kick her face in. I was very sorry he didn't.

As we approached the county road, I saw Sandy Hagar's pickup. My heart sank. Sandy and Ed Weeks, who lived in the neighborhood, had gone out for a Sunday drive and had seen one of our heifers dragging a rope. They both worked on ranches and they both knew what that meant. Fearing that someone had gotten hurt in a roping accident, they had gone looking for us. Their wives were in Ed's car, and they were scouting the north end of the pasture. I found out later that the wives ran into Kris on the road. She was bringing the pickup and trailer, and she was looking for us too.

At the very moment when Bill and I wanted nothing more than to crawl into a hole and disappear for a while, the entire neighborhood had mobilized and was trying to find us.

I told Sandy not to worry, apologized for stirring up the YL cattle, and told him what had happened. Well, I told him half the story. He and Ed had seen only one heifer dragging a rope, and I didn't tell him about the second one. Several months later, when Sandy and I were sitting around in his front yard, I told him the full story with all its gory details. He laughed.

I returned to Bill and the heifer. We continued driving her north toward the gate. Then she stopped in the shade of a little hackberry tree and wouldn't move. She put her tail to the tree and dared us to come get the rope. I rode in several times, and every time I reached for the rope she took a swipe at Reno. Finally I got the rope and we left her there and rode north to find the other heifer. The last time Bill had seen her, she had been running in that direction. Sure enough, we located her at the north end with one of Mark's cows and calves. After the wretch had gone through the fence into the middle pasture, then through the fence into Mark's pasture again, we roped her and dragged her into the middle pasture—which is exactly where we had started five and a half hours earlier.

There was a lesson in the experience, and it was branded into my memory. The lesson was that while it takes skill to rope an animal in the pasture, the real test of a cowboy comes when he has to get his rope back. Dabbing that loop on a cow brute's neck can be a lot of fun. Getting it back can be less than fun.

14
ANOTHER WRECK

With winter approaching in 1975, I wanted to move seven cow-calf pairs out of the west pasture, brand the calves, and turn the pairs into the big east. That would put all my branded calves into one pasture and all the dry cows in the middle and west.

Since I had been swapping out work with Tom Ellzey, I asked if he could come up and help me. He seemed a little puzzled that, if I only had seven calves to gather and brand, I would need him for a whole day. I reminded him that this was the Crown Ranch and that nothing was easy. On the evening of December 15, Tom and his wife, Janet, pulled in with two saddle horses. They spent the night, and the next morning we had a big breakfast of sausage, eggs, and homemade sourdough biscuits. After breakfast we saddled up Rusty for Tom, Frisco for Janet, and Reno for me, and loaded them into my gooseneck trailer. Then we all stuffed ourselves into the cab of the pickup—Tom, Janet, Kris, baby Scottie, and me—and Kris drove us out into the west pasture.

As we drove, I explained how I thought we should go about cutting off the pairs. Since these cattle would run from a horse, we would haul the horses to the feed ground on the north end of the pasture and call the cattle as though we were going to feed them. When they came in, we would have an opportunity to look them over and pick out the pairs. "We'll try to handle them gently," I said, repeating the absurdity I had uttered so many times. "But when your horse steps out of the trailer, you'd better be in the saddle and ready for some hard riding." Janet, who was accustomed to riding through the dog-gentle cows on the LZ Ranch, must have thought this was an exaggeration.

The cattle came in to the feed ground and we saw two of the pairs we wanted. We unloaded the horses and mounted up. The cattle began milling on the feed ground. We tried to ride around them and hold them in a bunch while we cut off the cows and calves. They broke into a run. We couldn't hold them, and they poured down the hill, heading south. We fell in behind them, whipping and spurring just to keep up. This was rough country, and before long our horses were jumping draws, ditches, and sagebrush. We stayed with the cattle for half a mile until I saw an opportunity to cut off one pair. I rode in and pushed them east. At about the same time Tom split off the other pair and brought them around. We threw them together and pushed them east and south. They probably wouldn't slow down until they hit the east fence a mile away.

I had told Kris to drive the pickup and trailer down to a place we called Eagle's Knob, and we met her there. It was a crisp morning and steam was rising from the sides of our horses when we loaded them into the trailer. Just to cut off two cow-calf pairs, we had broken a sweat on three horses.

From Eagle's Knob we drove deeper into the pasture, to a feed ground located just about in the center of it. After seeing how the north bunch had behaved, I doubted that

Tom Ellzey limbers up his roping arm in the corral near his home on Wolf Creek.

we could hold the herd while we cut them off. I decided to cut the pairs off as they came in to the feed ground. We unloaded the horses and I called the cattle. When a pair came in, we got around them and pushed them northward toward the home pens. It worked well, except that by the time we had cut off the fifth pair, the first ones were already a quarter mile away, heading north at a lope, while the others were strung out in between. I told Tom and Janet to fall in behind them and to pick up the two pairs we had cut off from the north bunch, and I would ride north and try to stop the lead cows.

I got on a ridge that ran the length of the pasture and put Reno into a lope. After a bit I spotted three cows and four calves running up the draw three hundred yards ahead of me. They were moving at such speed that, with Reno in a lope, I was losing ground. I dropped off the ridge so that they wouldn't see me, gave Reno his head, and galloped north to head them off. When I judged that I had caught up with them, I rode up on the ridge and showed myself. I thought this would haze them east where Tom and Janet would catch them and throw them in with the rest of the pairs they were bringing.

The lead cow in this bunch was a big, high-headed Charolais-crossbred. I don't know what it was about those yellow crossbred cows, but they had always been hard to handle. They were the worst runners and fighters on the ranch. This old crossbred hussy had set such a blistering pace that the two Hereford cows and four calves behind her were frothing at the mouth and had their tongues hanging out, yet she looked as though she could run all the way to Dodge City. I rode toward her and tried to ease her out of the draw and point her east. She wouldn't turn, so I just tried to keep up with her, hoping that sooner or later she would decide to go east.

They didn't stop or slow down until they reached the fence in front of the house, a mile north of the feed ground where we had cut them out. When the crossbred cow came to the fence, she tried to go west. Reno moved into her path and she tried another spot. Back and forth we went. Once, when Reno was making a quick turn, he hit a patch of mud and went down. My feet came out of the stirrups and I found myself sitting on the saddle horn and hanging onto his mane to keep from going overboard. I managed to stay on top, and Reno wallowed back to his feet and we held the cattle. I tried again to push them east, but the old yellow cow was ready to fight by then and I elected to hold them where they were. Tom and Janet would appear soon, and we would throw the two bunches together and drive them to the pens. But when I looked off into the pasture, I saw no sign of the Ellzeys.

I learned later that one of Tom's cows wouldn't drive. When he whipped her with his rope, she took a razoo at his horse. He roped her by the neck and threw a trip on her several times, but she still refused to move. Finally he gave up and went north to help Janet, who had followed the other cattle.

At last I caught a glimpse of Tom and Janet in the distance, and what I saw worried me. First one and then the other came flying over the top of the sandhills. In front of them thundered a herd of thirty cows which, apparently, they had encountered on the east side of the pasture, and into which their four pairs had mingled. When my little bunch of cattle saw the thirty head coming from the east, they threw up their heads and ran toward them. I stopped my horse on a little flat and waited for what I knew was coming.

How many times had I been in this position? In the stillness of morning, I could hear the thunder of hooves and the snapping of sagebrush as the cattle came toward me like a herd of buffalo. I felt the tension growing in my throat and a wrenching in my stomach. Old Reno watched the stampede drawing nearer and pranced on his front legs. He

had spent his entire life around these cattle and had faced
this kind of charge many times before.

When the cattle were a hundred feet away, I gave
Reno his head and he leaped to the attack. I yelled and
waved my arms, while Reno tore up the grass and sent mud
flying as he dashed, wheeled, leaped, and lunged, taking on
every cow that came his way. We were getting spread too
thin and we needed help. Out of the corner of my eye I saw
Tom moving up to help me. Good old Tom. When you got
in a storm, he was either there beside you or on his way.
We dashed back and forth, turning the cattle on the west
side and putting them into a mill. Janet held them on the
east and finally they came out of the mill and headed north
toward the pens. We followed them in and shut the gate behind them. We dismounted and loosened the cinches on
our lathered horses. Rusty and Frisco, who were not accustomed to this kind of madness, must have thought they had
died and gone to hell. Tom and I joked about it, saying that
it was just a typical gather on the Crown Ranch. But Janet,
who had just gotten her first taste of wild cattle, was ap-
palled.

"Erickson," she said in her Toledo accent, "anyone
who'd work around these cattle every day has to be crazy or
have a lot of guts."

I assured her that it was the former, and Tom added
his testimony.

The cattle were so hot and stirred up it took Tom and
me two hours to pair up and cut off the cows and calves.
When we quit for lunch at one o'clock, we discovered that
the electricity had gone off some time that morning and still
had not come back on. Kris and Janet had to load the food
and dishes into the car and drive down to cook the meal on
Geneva Hagar's stove. Finally we got our lunch at three.

By the time we finished the branding, the evening
shadows were growing long. It had been a long, hard day,
but we had gotten the work done and all we had left to do

was to load the cattle into the trailer and haul them over to the big east pasture. Loading Crown-branded cattle was never an easy chore, since by the time you got them to the corrals they were choused and ready to fight. But we got them loaded, and I closed the trailer gate with a feeling of accomplishment. Then I heard Tom roar, "Oh my God, the front gate's open."

I couldn't believe it. I had forgotten to close the side door on the front of the trailer, and now the cattle were trotting across the horse pasture. I said to heck with them, I'd haul them tomorrow. We laughed it off. At least the work was done and the day was over.

Well, almost. As Tom was loading Rusty and Frisco, he discovered that he had lost four of the seven leaf springs on the left side of his stock trailer. It was dark now, and the cold of winter night had set in. We found a jack and some tools and went to work. I held a flashlight in my shivering hands while Tom made some temporary repairs that would keep the frame off the axle until he got home. Finally, at nine o'clock, Tom and Janet started back to Wolf Creek.

All of this to brand seven calves. On the Crown Ranch, nothing was simple.

HORSES

15
BLACKJACK AND MOMMA MARE

When I arrived on the Crown Ranch in January 1974, I found four horses in the trap around the barn: two geldings and two mares. I didn't know anything about these horses, whether they were good cow horses or even broke to ride, their quirks, their names, nothing.

A good bronc stomper would have solved the problem by throwing a saddle on them and testing them out one by one. I wasn't a bronc stomper. These were all full-grown horses, several of them big and stout, and I wasn't anxious to get myself thrown into the next township just to satisfy my curiosity. I decided to move slowly and to wait for warmer weather. In the meantime, I scouted the ranch and rode the pastures on my own horse, Dollarbill, whom I had brought with me to the ranch. Dollarbill was not a great horse, but he had the enormous advantage of being calm, friendly, and predictable.

In time, as I met cowboys who had worked on the

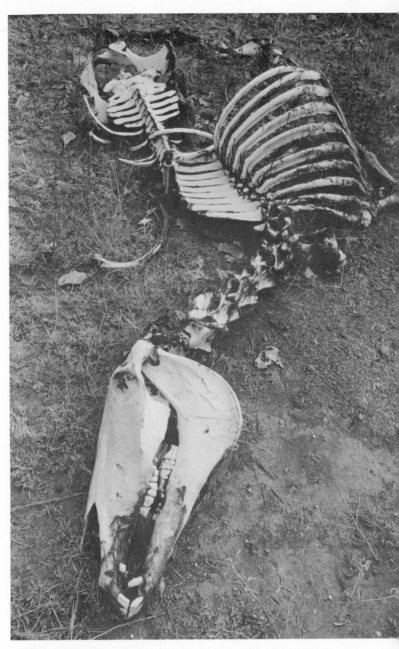

This is all that remains of a ranch horse that died of old age.

ranch and became better acquainted with the neighbors, I learned more about the horses and pieced together a vague profile of each. I learned that the bay gelding Reno was broke and gentle and had been used as a cow horse. I learned that Momma Mare was a registered thoroughbred, had once run on the track, and had permanently gimped a hind leg several years before when she had kicked the back end out of a horse trailer. About the other two horses, Gypsy and Blackjack, I knew very little. They were full brother and sister, both out of Momma Mare and a big quarter horse stud. Gypsy, the mare, was close to six years old, and Blackjack, the gelding, was eight or nine. No one could tell me how far they had been taken in training, whether they were broke to ride, green broke, or untrained.

In time, I tested every one of the horses and made decisions about their future on the ranch. Reno and Gypsy stayed as long as I did. Blackjack and Momma Mare didn't.

After I learned that Momma Mare was crippled, I never even considered riding her. And I didn't trust her either. She had a wicked streak, and I handled her as little as possible. I kept her as a brood mare and let her run in the pasture. In August 1974, I bred her to Mark Mayo's Arabian stallion, and the following July she had a filly foal named Calipso. In the spring of 1976, after I had weaned the foal, I recommended to the bank that we sell the mare. Keith Good told me to go ahead, and I hauled her to the livestock sale in Guymon.

As you might expect, after Momma Mare had destroyed a horse trailer and crippled herself, she was a little goofy about trailers. Getting her loaded for the trip to Guymon was a major chore, and I couldn't have done it without Mark's help. On the way to Guymon I felt as though I were hauling gunpowder, and I kept waiting for her to kick the middle gate out of the trailer. But she didn't, and we made the trip without any trouble. When we got

there, I led her into the yards and was removing the halter
from her head when something spooked her. Maybe it was
the wind, a gum wrapper, a weed, a strange sound. It could
have been anything. She was just waiting for an excuse to
booger.

She exploded, knocked me down, ran over the top of
me, and began dashing around the pen. I scrambled to the
fence and got out of her way. By this time three of the cowboys in the yard had come over to see what was going on,
and together we watched as she did her utmost to destroy a
gate made of two-by-six lumber and a pen made of
two-inch pipe. Had it not been a substantial pen, she might
have done it. She kicked it, struck it with her front feet, and
rammed it with her chest.

If the cowboys had not come over to watch, I would
have simply walked away and let her sell with the halter on.
But these three cowboys, all young rakehells with big cowboy hats and lips pouched with snuff, were waiting to see
what I would do—or, as they conceived it, if I had guts
enough to step into the pen with her and try again to remove the halter. It was an unspoken dare.

There was no good reason why I should have cared
what these boys thought. They appeared to be the typical
coffee shop and sale barn cowboys. Every little town in the
American Southwest has dozens of them. For them, cowboying is not a job or a profession but a style of life. They
may work at a gas station six days a week, but on Friday, at
the livestock sale, they are pure undiluted cowboys. Many
of them dabble in rodeo or team roping on the side, and a
few may even win enough prize money to pay their snuff
bill.

They were waiting to see if I would step into the pen
with Momma Mare.

The smart man would have cashed in his chips and
gone home, too happy to be rid of the mare to worry at all
about giving away five dollars' worth of halter. But I

couldn't give those little snuff-dippers something to talk about all afternoon. I could just hear them: "By God, if she'd a-been mine, I'da went in thur and kicked her sumbitchin' guts out. I'da forefooted her and throwed a trip on her and stood her on her sumbitchin' nose and tied her down. I'da whupped her with a trace chain. I'da tuned her up with a two-by-four." Acting on what was probably a childish impulse, I decided to get the halter.

The boys waited and watched. Momma Mare was putting on quite a show. She unloaded on the gate three times, and I expected it to come off its hinges. Just as she was about to settle down, an empty potato chip package blew across the pen and she went around again. Finally she quit. By this time she had raised such a racket and such a cloud of dust that everyone in the yards was wondering what in God's name that was in pen number five. I gave her a minute to settle down, then eased off the fence and walked toward her, talking quietly. My plan was to catch her while she was tired, take the halter off very gently, and then scram before she blew the cork again.

I was lucky. I caught her, unbuckled the halter, walked slowly but very straight to the nearest fence, bid the cowboys on the fence good afternoon, and headed for the pickup. As I walked away, I heard her hooves ringing the pipe corral like church bells. I indulged myself in an inward smile. She's all yours now, cowboys, and lots of luck.

At the same time I decided to sell Momma Mare, I suggested that we sell the gelding Blackjack, and for the same reason: horses are expensive to keep, and on a working cattle ranch, those which don't earn their keep don't deserve to stay. I had kept Blackjack around for a year and a half, hoping that I could work with him and make a horse out of him. He was a handsome devil, coal black, well muscled, and big enough to pull a house down. I would have been proud to ride him. But he had one huge liability that overshadowed his strength and beauty: he had gone too

long without being broke and used, and at nine years of age
he was just too old. Also, since I had already had several
bad experiences with his female relatives, I had formed a
bad opinion of his family.

My relationship with Blackjack was brief and, I think,
rather interesting. I had always dreaded the day when I
would start working with him. He was so big and so stout I
couldn't help calculating how high and far he could throw
me if he ever decided he wanted to. Most horses are broke
at the age of two, or sometimes even sooner, before they
have gotten their full growth. A colt can buck and buck
hard, but the rider stands a good chance of staying aboard
and shutting him down. Blackjack was nine years old and
weighed twelve or thirteen hundred pounds. He was stout
enough to throw me into the next county. But he was such
a beautiful beast I hated to sell him.

One day I decided that it was time to try him out. I
had run out of excuses. I ran him into a pen and approached
him with a bridle. He didn't want to be caught, and took
evasive action. But I hemmed him into a corner. He took the
bit without a struggle. Then I threw a saddle on him to see
what he would do. He winced when I tightened the cinch,
but it wasn't what you would call a bad reaction. Clearly,
he had been under saddle before. I led him around with the
saddle on for a while, giving him plenty of chances to cut
loose if it made him nervous. He didn't react.

When I worked with a new horse, I proceeded a step at
a time, and each step brought me closer to the moment
when I would have to climb on his back. How quickly I
moved from one stage to another was determined by how I
felt about the horse. It was strictly a matter of intuition.
With Blackjack, the empirical evidence said that he had
passed all the tests, yet my intuition kept sending up warning flags and telling me that I was moving toward trouble.
There was something about the horse that bothered me. He
submitted to my tests, but without feeling or enthusiasm.

He just stood there, and I couldn't tell by looking at him what he was thinking. I sensed an air of silent resentment in him, but I kept telling myself that I was imagining it. I moved on to the next stage.

Finally I was sitting in the saddle—and for the sake of honesty in literature, I will say that my palms were sweating. There he stood. He wasn't fighting, but he wasn't relaxed either. He knew I was up there, and he was thinking about it. Well, I had to go on to the next step. I nudged him with my boot heels and told him to get up. He started walking around the pen, but it wasn't an easy walk. He seemed to be counting every step, almost as though he intended to make me pay for every one of them.

I had succeeded in making him move forward, and now I tried to turn him. I reined him to the left. He stopped in his tracks. I pulled harder on the rein and nudged him with my heels. He didn't move. He set the muscles in his neck and pulled against me. We stood there for several minutes. The harder I pulled on his head, the stiffer his neck became, until I felt that I had my bridle and reins attached to a tree trunk.

The first rule of horse training is that you cannot allow the horse to defeat you, impose his will on you, or disobey a reasonable command. If he does, and if this pattern is established early in the training period, the time will come when it becomes not only annoying, but dangerous as well. Sometimes a cowboy's health depends on the obedience of his horse.

I had given Blackjack the command to turn. He refused to move. I either had to force him to turn, and to do it right then, or else give up. I could have put on a pair of spurs. I could have whipped him with a strap or a stick. I had used all the gentle tricks I knew and they hadn't worked. All that remained was a direct confrontation of wills.

I sat there in the saddle for several minutes, wondering

what I should do. I looked at the massive neck, shoulders, and hindquarters on the beast and calculated the physical force that could be generated by those rippling muscles. I admitted that I was afraid of him, and I remembered something I had heard from a man who had spent his entire life around horses: "If you ever reach the point where you're afraid of a horse, you'd better get rid of him—fast." I stepped down, led Blackjack to the barn, pulled off the saddle, and turned him out to pasture. The next time I handled him, it was to load him into the trailer so I could haul him to the horse sale in Woodward, Oklahoma.

I never regretted the decision. Blackjack defeated me, and I accepted it. Maybe if I had challenged him with spurs, he would have submitted and gone on to become a fine ranch horse. Maybe he bluffed me out. That was fine with me. I knew my limits, and I knew that he was too much horse for me. I was content to leave it to a better man to call his bluff.

16
GYPSY

The third member of this family of outlaws was Blackjack's sister, Gypsy. Her coloring fell somewhere between a bay and a black, and she had a splash of white on her face. She had good length and height and probably weighed eleven hundred pounds.

As to her looks, I was never able to decide whether she was handsome or ugly. My opinion of her beauty seemed to changed from week to week. There were times when I thought she was as homely as mud. Her face seemed too long, her neck too thin, and her hooves as big as washtubs. On good grass, she tended to develop a pot belly, which in turn made her hindquarters appear underdeveloped. Yet there were other times when I was struck by her good looks. In the spring, when her coat had slicked off and begun to shine, when she was in working shape and under saddle, she could turn heads at a spring roundup and inspire the cowboys to make such poetic comments as "That ain't a bad lookin' murr you're ridin'."

Mike Harter, David Hagar, and I (right to left) had spent a very hot afternoon pulling the rods out of a windmill. When we returned to the barn, we stripped off and bailed into the stock tank to cool off. Bill Ellzey was in the area and dropped by for a visit. When we saw him coming, we decided to greet him with the pose "hear no evil, see no evil, speak no evil," a pose more often associated with monkeys than with ranch hands.

I suppose the best way of describing the difference between Blackjack and Gypsy is to say that Blackjack resembled a thug, while in Gypsy I detected a certain awkward innocence that could be rather appealing. Now that I think about it, their names were appropriate to their personalities: Blackjack, a concealed weapon made to bust heads, and Gypsy, a creature of changing mood and temperament who could charm you around the campfire and then try to murder you in your bed.

When I began working with Gypsy in early May 1974, I started from scratch and handled her as though she were a green colt. I put a halter on her head and spent the first several hours in ground training, which means that I led her around the pen and issued voice commands to "get up," "whoa," and "back." I brushed her and handled her, picked up her feet and climbed on her bareback. My impression after the first day was that she was gentle and affectionate, that she had probably been green broke at one time, and that she would make a good mount.

About a week later, I decided it was time to put a bit in her mouth, and it was then that I became aware of her darker side. She didn't want to take the bit. For half an hour she jumped and boogered and pushed me away with her nose, a habit that began to annoy me after a while, since she had enough strength in her head and neck to lift me off the ground and throw me into the fence. She did it once too often, my temper flared, and I kicked her in the belly.

To someone who has never worked around ranch animals, kicking a horse in the belly may seem a severe and cruel form of punishment. As a matter of fact, the cowboy stands a much better chance of breaking his toe than of hurting the horse. Kicking a horse sounds bad, but it really isn't.

With horses, there is a difference between cruelty and punishment. Some men seem to take pride in thumping on a horse. Without good cause, they will whip him with a piece of lumber or chain, jerk the bits in his mouth, or even spur him with sharpened rowels. That kind of behavior is not only shameful, it is counter-productive. A good cowboy has respect for his horses. He takes care of them and they take care of him. He has no use for cruelty, but he will not hesitate to discipline his horse, and sometimes this calls for stern measures. The difference between cruelty and punishment does not lie in severity or degree, but in purpose: punishment is administered with a goal in mind and for a reason, while cruelty is gratuitous and purposeless.

After I kicked Gypsy, she took the bit. It was a straight curb bit and it made her so nervous and uncomfortable that I decided to try a snaffle. A snaffle is a type of bit with a mouthpiece that is hinged in the middle. It puts less pressure on a horse's tender mouth than a curb, and it is often used on green horses as a training bit. The snaffle didn't bother her. She wasn't as nervous now, and toward the end of May, after I had worked with her on the ground, thrown a saddle on her, and ridden her around the pen, I decided the time had come to take her for a ride in the pasture.

I walked her the first two hundred yards, then kicked her up into a trot. She was doing so well I kicked her on up to a short lope. Stretching out her long legs, she covered a lot of ground in this gait, and I was pleased that her lope was very smooth. I had these pleasant thoughts in mind when a locust flew up in front of her nose, buzzing and flapping its wings. She bogged her head, kicked up her hind legs, and blasted me out of the saddle before I even knew what was happening.

Rodeo riders have one big advantage over ranch cowboys. In rodeo, when a man climbs on a horse, he knows what that horse is going to do when the gate swings open. He expects a bronc and he's prepared for it. The poor cowboy, on the other hand, rarely has any advance warning when his mount blows up.

I had just begun to relax and enjoy the ride. I had released my grip on the saddle horn and was not sitting deep in the saddle. When Gypsy fired, my feet came out of the stirrups and I flew straight out of my seat. After a short flight, I fell back onto the saddle, was launched once again, and crashed right back over the saddle. She put me away on the third jump. My feet passed my head and kept going. I flew through the air upside-down, with the soles of my boots reflecting the afternoon sun, and crashed face-first into a clump of sagebrush. When I raised up, my glasses were sitting on my front teeth and Gypsy was bucking across the pasture. I had a few sagebrush etchings on my face, but otherwise I wasn't hurt. When Gypsy quit bucking, I walked up to her and caught her.

According to the Code of the West, you can't quit a horse after he has piled you. You have to get right back on. Perhaps more important than the code is the fact that if you don't get back on, you have to walk home. So I climbed back into the saddle and pointed Gypsy toward the house. When the next locust flew up in front of her, I was ready. She didn't even flinch.

I had planned to ride her every day to work the edge off her, but a few days later I broke a bone in my right hand and had to wear a plaster cast for the next four weeks. (I spoke earlier of the hazards of kicking a horse. I slugged a calf.) I didn't want to ride the mare with a cast on my hand, but in early June I decided that I ought to work with her on the ground, just to keep her gentle.

I caught her and led her into the alley in front of the barn. As I was drawing up the cinch, she spooked at something and went berserk. I dived into the barn to get out of her way, but not before she had stomped on my foot. She threw a bucking fit in the alley. The saddle, which I had not managed to fasten at the cinch, went under her belly and caused her to pitch all the more, and she didn't quit until she had planted it in the dirt.

The outburst annoyed me, not only because my foot

hurt, but also because there had been no reason for it. For all I knew, she had spooked at a mouse or a grasshopper. If her nerves were that fragile, then she needed some nerve tonic. I didn't intend to ride a mare that was going to buck every time she saw a grasshopper. I caught her, saddled her again, and led her into a pen. She was as taut as a spring and was looking all around for devils. I never turned my back on her, and when I had to stand close to her, I kept one hand on her side so that if she erupted again I could push off her body and get away.

Since she wanted to play rodeo, I decided to give her a whole afternoon of it. Very carefully I tied gunny sacks to the stirrups and eased away. She stood quivering for a moment, then, when she moved and saw the sacks out of the corner of her eye, she blew up. Around and around she went. When she finally quit, I was waiting with more nerve tonic. I tied tin cans to the saddle, to her ears and tail, slapped her on the butt, and told her to get after it. While she bucked around the pen, I stood in the middle, yelling and waving my hat. She quit bucking, and I threw rocks at her and got her started again. She bucked until she didn't have a hump left in her back.

I kept her in the pen for two days, dragging cans and sacks around with her. She was quite a comical sight, looking as though she had had a collision with a garbage truck.

When the cast was removed from my hand, I started riding her again. I rode her several hours every day, through the roughest sandhill country on the ranch. She improved a little more each day, and once again it appeared that I was going to make a saddle mare out of her.

Then, toward the end of June, I wasn't able to ride her for two days, and the next time I saddled her up I could see that she had gone backward. She was jumpy. She had the old devils inside her again. I sacked her out and rode her hard for two hours and had, I thought, worked all the mischief out of her. As we were walking up a sand draw on the

way home, a locust flew up in front of her. Three jumps
and she put me to bed.

I rode her through the summer and she did very well.
I began roping off her. She showed fine speed and endurance, and I appreciated her smooth lope. She didn't have
any cow sense at all, but I figured that would come with
time. Since old Reno, my number one cow horse, was
getting up in years, I began grooming Gypsy to move into
his place.

I had no more trouble with her until October of that
year. David Hagar, Sandy and Geneva's son, was home for
a visit, and he and I went out riding in the west pasture. We
were loping across some brushy sandhills, and as we came
to the top of a hill, I saw a badger hole directly in my path.
I tried to check Gypsy, but it was already too late. She
didn't see the hole, fell into it with her left front leg, and
went down. As she was going down, I flew out of the saddle and over her head. When I hit the ground, I looked back
to see if she was going to fall on top of me. It was just a matter of curiosity, since I couldn't have gotten out of the way.
Fortunately, she didn't come on over, but she did roll over
my leg. The swell of the saddle caught me on the inside of
the thigh, and for an instant I felt a thousand pounds of
pressure on that one spot. Then she wallowed up,
somehow missed stepping on me with her washtub feet,
and started bucking. I got out of the wreck with nothing
but a big, ugly bruise.

It's hard to say whether or not you should blame a
horse for falling into a hole. Maybe it's a freak accident that
will never happen again, or maybe it's a sign of awkward
feet, poor eyesight, or lack of intelligence, in which case it
might happen again. You can argue about it, but there was
no question about the impression this incident left on me.
It added to the feeling I had had all along, and which would
increase with time, that for one reason or another, Gypsy
was not quite predictable or trustworthy. Riding her, you

could never relax. You found yourself watching for holes
and tensing up every time a locust flew. For that reason I
didn't ride her at all that winter.

The following May, when roundup season rolled
around, I found myself riding Reno. Gypsy had been running in the pasture for six months and had gone back to her
wild ways, and I wasn't anxious to tangle with her again.
Nor did I relish the thought of trying to load her into a
trailer at five-thirty on a roundup morning. Loading a
snaky horse in the dark was not my idea of a good time.

Around the middle of May I was helping the McFarlands round up a big pasture on the Beaver River. Reno fell
into some quicksand and injured his leg so badly that I
wasn't sure he would ever be sound again. When I got back
to the ranch that afternoon, I faced an unpleasant task. I
turned Reno out to pasture and ran Gypsy in. Tomorrow
morning I would have to load her in the dark, then ride her
all day at the McFarland roundup. If I had trouble loading
her, I would be late for the roundup. I had never in my life
been late to a roundup. If she piled me in McFarlands' pasture, I would be humiliated. I had never in my life been
piled in the presence of a crew.

I had four hours of daylight left in which to break her,
knock the edge off her, and get her ready to load and ride
the following morning. Working against that time limit, I
wasn't in any mood to put up with her foolishness. As I approached her with the bridle in my hand, I must have
looked about as friendly as the Grim Reaper.

She behaved as though she had never seen a man before. When I put her in a corner and walked toward her,
she hugged the fence, turned her rump toward me, and
wouldn't allow me to catch her head. When I approached
her from one side, she would bolt away in the other direction. She was determined that I wasn't going to catch her. I
was determined that I would. She had always been a little
hard to catch, but now she was worse than I had ever seen

her before. I tried three or four times to approach her, and when it didn't work, I went for a catch rope. The next time she bolted and ran, I dropped the loop over her head. I don't suppose she had ever been roped before, and she fought like a tiger. When I walked up the rope toward her head, she stood up on her hind legs and struck at me. This shocked me at first, and then it made me mad. She had violated the rules and had escalated our struggle from a simple difference of opinion into an open brawl. We would no longer abide by the code of ladies and gentlemen.

When I finally got control of her head, I threw a half hitch over her nose and led her to a big stout post in the corner of the pen. I tied her to the post and snubbed her up as close as I could. She went back on all four feet and fought the rope with all her strength. If I had not thrown the half hitch over her nose, if she had only had the rope around her neck, she might have uprooted the post or killed herself in the struggle. But as she fought against the rope, it tightened down on her nose. The harder she fought, the more it hurt. She gave up and I put a halter on her head.

I had won the first round, but I knew that she was still full of devils. If I had saddled her up and tried to ride her at this point, she would have piled me. She still wanted to buck and fight. Fine. I was going to let her buck until she wanted to quit, and then I was going to make her buck some more. I was going to torment her until she was so tired she couldn't hump her back one more time.

She didn't know what I had in mind, and she watched with wide eyes as I eased my catch rope around her flanks. We had never played this game before, and she didn't know what to expect. I had to be very careful running the rope around her flanks. She was quivering like a time bomb and kicking at the rope with her hind feet. Reaching under her belly for the honda-end of the rope, I had to dodge her shots and stay loose enough that I could jump backward if she tried to run over me. When I got the rope around her flanks, I held it in my right hand and the halter rope in my left.

I jerked the lariat rope. The noose tightened around her flanks. She snorted and blew up. She dropped her head and kicked up her heels, and away we went. With the halter rope I could control her head and keep her moving in a circle. Around and around she bucked, until she had had enough. I jerked the flank rope, and with a grunt, she joined the rodeo again.

This must have gone on for forty-five minutes. Every time she stopped, I jerked the flank rope and made her pitch some more. At last she just stood there, heaving for breath and sweating and blinking her eyes. I led her to the barn and saddled her up. I rode her hard through the sand-hills in the middle pasture and raked her with spurs every time she tried to stop. When we came back to the barn, it was getting dark. I took her to the stock trailer and told her to load. When she balked, I beat on her with a stick until she loaded.

Four hours after the session began, Gypsy was broke to load and ride. It had been a brawl from start to finish, and I had come out the winner. The next morning she loaded into the trailer and performed very well at the McFarland roundup. She was always a good mare, once you got the devils out of her, but she never stayed broke. If you left her in the pasture for a week, you had it all to do over again.

Gypsy was a dangerous horse. I had known it all along but had decided to put up with her simply because, with Reno out of commission, I didn't have anything else to ride. Dollarbill was a nice gentle horse, but he just didn't have enough endurance for a long, hard day. I told myself that if I were careful around Gypsy, if I sacked her out before I rode her, I could get by until we could either buy another horse or bring up a colt to take her place. I figured I could put up with her for another year or two. But at my spring roundup in 1975 I had a narrow escape that changed my mind.

This was the notorious Broken Leg Roundup. The morning of the first day we set out to gather the middle pasture. I was mounted on Gypsy, and since I wanted to put a sweat on her and give her a hard workout, I went to the back side of the pasture where the country was rough and sandy. With me I took Kris, who was riding Dollarbill, and Jimmy Smith. Jimmy was riding the black gelding that, the next morning, would break his leg. When we got into the sandhills, we split up and spread out.

By this time I had a quart of coffee working in my bladder, and at my first opportunity I rode behind a sandhill and got down to answer the call. As I was stepping down, I hung a spur in the back cinch. Gypsy must have been waiting for a goblin to jump out of the brush. She rolled her eyes and stamped her feet and began moving away from me. Since I had only one leg on the ground, I had to hop toward her to keep from being pulled off my feet. As long as I kept my feet, I had a chance of reaching my spur and pulling it out of the cinch. If I went down, I knew that I could be dragged. I had to hold on to the reins and keep my feet. But my hopping only contributed to Gypsy's fright, and each time I hopped toward her, she lurched farther away. At last she got me down, jerked the reins out of my hand, and started running, dragging me with her.

I was frightened at the prospect of being dragged, but I was also disgusted that it was being done to me by this particular mare. I hated to give the wench the pleasure of dragging my carcass all over the ranch.

But luck was with me that morning. After a short sleigh ride through the brush, the spur slipped over the heel of my boot and I rolled to a stop. Kris caught the mare and brought her back, and I went ahead and finished the roundup season on her, but shortly thereafter I contacted Bill Ellzey and talked him into selling Suds, his gray horse.

The moment Suds arrived on the ranch, Gypsy's career as a cowhorse came to an end. I never rode her again. She had piled me three times, rolled on me once, and dragged me once. I figured that was enough.

Looking back, I marvel that I put up with her as long as I did. I guess it was a bit like a bad love affair. You learn to cope and adjust, you tolerate the intolerable, you forget that life is too short to spend in torment. It is a hellish experience, but when the day of parting comes, when the yoke is lifted, the air is fresher and the day more beautiful than you had ever imagined.

17
RENO

Old Reno was a handsome devil. His breeding was half Arabian and half quarter horse. He was stouter than most Arabian geldings but smaller than a quarter horse, and his body gave the impression of sturdiness but not overpowering strength. If you wanted to describe him in human terms, you might say that he resembled a sprinter more than a football player, a gymnast more than a wrestler. He was a light bay in color, had a short head and big dewy eyes, and one stocking foot.

In temperament, he was dog-gentle, but unlike his Arabian forebears, he had no affection for the human race. Only once during my four years with Reno did I get the feeling that he liked me. He didn't nuzzle or rub or come running to greet me. Most often he gave me the impression that I was a nuisance, neither better nor worse than the other two-legged creatures who had imposed on his time and intruded into his privacy. He was strictly professional in his approach, and his attitude seemed to be that if you could

Erickson hisself.

make him do something, fine, he would do it well. But if you couldn't make him, he certainly wasn't going to volunteer anything or assist you in any way.

I got a taste of this side of Reno the first time I tried to catch him in the horse pasture. Carrying a bridle over my shoulder, I walked toward the horses who were grazing near the barn. The other three horses came up to sniff and say hello. After all, I was the guy who fed them, and that was worth something. Reno remained aloof and kept his distance. He didn't even look directly at me. But when I passed the other horses by and approached him, when it became obvious that I intended to catch him, he trotted away and headed for the backside of the horse pasture.

I soon learned that if I wanted to get Reno into the pens, the best way of doing it was to pretend that I didn't have any interest in him. When I appeared at the barn door with a bucket of oats and whistled, the other horses would come at a run. Reno would either not come in at all or would bring up the rear. When I led the other horses into the pen and poured out the feed, he would still be standing in the pasture, watching to see what I would do. If I stayed around the barn he wouldn't move. If I got into the pickup and drove away, he would throw his head and tail into the air and gallop for the feed trough. Then I would jump out of the pickup, sneak around the back side of the barn, and close the gate while he was eating.

You had to be shrewd around old Reno. If you were ever in a hurry and needed to get him up right away, if you ever tipped your hand and let him sense what you had in mind, he would either walk away with a smirking air or make a dash for the back side of the pasture, laughing, it seemed, as you sputtered with rage. The madder you grew the more he enjoyed the game. At the very times when you would have gotten down on your knees and begged him to come into the pens, he remained haughty and aloof.

In the pen, when you approached him with the bridle,

he would whirl and dash around the fence, and if you didn't know the horse you might very well think he had never been bridled before and was half-dangerous. But this was strictly show business, and in time I learned to approach him on a mature level, so to speak, as one professional to another. I would point a finger at him and say, "Reno, I outsmarted you. It was a fair game and you lost. Now take the bit like a man and let's get on with our work." He could never resist this appeal to his professional pride, and he would drop the bluff, stand his ground, and take the bit.

Once bridled, he became as efficient and predictable as a machine. There was no more bluff or monkey business. From then on, he was Reno, Professional Ranch Horse.

He performed his work with a rare combination of skill, natural ability, and courage. His specialty was chasing wild cattle over sandhills, and for this type of work he was as perfect as a horse could be. He combined quick reflexes with tremendous acceleration, top-end speed, and endurance. And he was sure-footed, which is a nice quality to find in a horse that likes to run.

I remember the day I learned to trust his feet. We had gone over to help Mark Mayo round up his east pasture. A cow broke from the herd and was making a dash for freedom. Reno saw what needed to be done, took the bit in his teeth, and started after her in a gallop. Since I wasn't familiar with the pasture, I was a little uneasy about moving so fast. But Reno seemed to know what he was doing, and I gave him his head.

All at once a ravine loomed up in front of us probably five feet deep and ten feet across. Stopping the horse was out of the question. Reno didn't have much of a whoa, and I might just as easily have tried to stop a truck. He didn't slow down or even break his stride. He plunged into the ditch, hit the center with his front feet, lunged forward and upward with his back legs, scaled the opposite bank, and kept right on going. Had my thighs not caught the saddle swells in the midst of these gymnastics, I wouldn't have made it. By the time we reached firm ground, I had lost the reins and stirrups and was a-horseback only in the vaguest sense.

After that experience I stopped trying to guide Reno through tight spots and rough ground. From then on I gave him his head and let him worry about it while I tried to stay in the saddle.

I remember Reno as the most daring, exhilarating horse I ever sat on. But he was also the roughest. The first time I took him out into the pasture and put him through his paces, I thought he was bucking. I returned home that evening with a whiplashed neck and a grinding headache. It was only when I rode him a second and third time that I began to absorb the awful truth: Reno wasn't bucking; that was his normal gait. I told Kris that Reno was the only horse I had ever ridden that could lope across the pasture and sprain your ankle in the stirrup.

He was a great horse, a magnificent beast, but you paid for your ride with pounds of flesh and by enduring physical abuse. He was hot-blooded and aggressive and he loved action. He moved with a kind of jabbing, thrusting motion, pivoting on his hind legs and driving his front legs into the ground. I think maybe his center of gravity did not lie in the middle of his body but more toward the rear, so that at any moment he could drive his front legs into the ground and make a ninety-degree turn. It was very nice when we were cutting cattle, but he moved that way all the time, and after a while the constant pounding began to take its toll. Reno had two smooth gaits: a walk and a gallop. Everything in between resembled an earthquake. In order to stay in the saddle, you had to use your knees and legs to grip his sides. After several hours of this kind of riding, the hair on your calves was rolled in little balls and you had sores from the tops of your boots to your knees. And if you had to ride him again the next day, you got sores on top of sores.

The first spring roundup season I spent with Reno, I had to cut the tops out of a pair of socks and tape them to my calves. Otherwise the galls would have become unbearable. When I was riding him hard and regularly, the insides of my calves looked as though they had been shaved clean with a razor.

And he had other shortcomings. The very qualities that made him such an outstanding roundup horse made him one of the world's poorest roping horses. He was high-headed and had an iron jaw. When you gave him his head and fell in behind a calf, he would lunge forward, catch up with the calf in a short distance, and then blow right past him. He never figured out what roping was all about and he never paid the slightest attention to the calf, and that gut-rupturing stride of his made it all but impossible to concentrate on the rope.

In May of 1974, Reno and I went down to the YL Ranch to help Mark round up the river pasture. In this big sandhill pasture old Reno was in his element. No hill was too high, no ground too rough, no cow too fast to wear him down. When we penned the last bunch of cattle after three hours of hard work, he was ready for more. I was proud to be riding the old horse, and I knew that I was well mounted.

When we reached the corrals, we closed the outside gates, pushed the cattle into the east pen, and left the horses tied along the fence in the west pen. Then we began separating the cows and calves, cutting the cows and bulls into the west pen. That done, Mark rode into the herd and roped a heifer calf that had sneaked past the man on the gate. He dragged the heifer back into the east pen with the other calves. I was standing in the west pen, watching Terry Dean as he flanked the calf down to get the rope off its neck, when I heard a commotion among the cattle to my right.

Two of Mark's big, horned Hereford bulls, finding themselves in close quarters and sharing the same territory, had decided to fight it out. They crashed into one another in the center of the pen. They bellowed and pawed the ground and a cloud of red dust rose around them. Grown cows were knocked to the ground and sent flying against the fence. A bull fight in a crowded pen can be dangerous, since the bulls will run over anything that gets in their way, and I wasted no time climbing the fence. All at once one of the bulls gave up the fight, broke to his right, and tried to escape the victor, who fell right in behind him with head down and horns out.

In his attempt to escape, the first bull stampeded down the south fence—where four horses were standing tied. He plowed right into the middle of them. The air filled with sounds of violence: the bellow of the bulls, the thunder of hooves, the shriek of horses, and the crash of steel as animals flew into the landing mat fence. Above the dust I could see the heads of the horses, their eyes white with fear and their headstalls, bits, and reins flying to pieces.

Then, above the clamor, I heard one of the cowboys yell, "He got one of the horses!" I squinted my eyes and looked toward the horses but could see nothing because of the dust. Several of the horses had been knocked down and were struggling to regain their feet. Then, through the fog of dust, I saw the horse. A broken headstall hung around his neck. He was walking on wobbly legs. Dark red blood gushed from a hole in his throat. He was coming toward me. It was Reno.

Reno was an impersonal, unfriendly horse, and he had never shown any affection for me. But now he did. This was the only time in my four years with him that he ever acknowledged a bond between us. He came to me, and I knew why: he thought he was dying, and for reasons which I don't pretend to understand, he wanted to be with me.

Ranching is an unsentimental business. Horses come and go. You observe the process of birth and death every day. But I wanted to put my arms around Reno's neck and comfort him like a child. Instead I placed my hand over the hole in his throat in a pitiful attempt to slow the flow of blood. Or maybe I did it just to remove the wound from my sight. In a matter of seconds the blood was running between my fingers.

When Mark saw what had happened, he jumped off his horse and came at a run. He had studied veterinary medicine in college and was an accomplished amateur horse and cow doctor. He gently pushed me out of the way and examined the wound. After probing it with his finger, he said that the bull's horn had penetrated four or five inches into Reno's throat and, he feared, had severed the jugular vein. He turned to me with a grim face. "John, the old horse may not make it." I nodded.

Mark traced out the vein with his finger and applied pressure with the heel of his hand four inches above the wound. The flow of blood slowed to a trickle. Then he ordered his son Steve to drive to the house and call the vet in Beaver. "If we can keep him alive until the vet gets here," Mark said to the cowboys who had gathered around, "maybe he can sew up the vein and save him."

Then he told me to lead Reno to the stock tank and try to get him to drink. He had lost a lot of blood and needed to get some fluid into his system. I led him to the tank, and while Mark continued to apply pressure to the vein, the horse took a drink. I was surprised. When I had first seen the wound, I expected him to be dead in a matter of minutes.

Applying pressure to the vein proved to be strenuous work, and when Mark's arms gave out, his place was taken by another cowboy. Working in shifts, we held the vein for

forty-five minutes. At last we saw the vet's pickup coming
down the road toward us, sending up a plume of red dust in
his path. When Doc Chockley was there beside us, the
cowboy "on duty" stepped back and we all waited to see
what would happen. The bleeding had almost stopped.
Doc inspected the wound and looked up with a smile.
"There's nothing I can do for this old horse. He's too tough
to die." The vein had been cut but not severed, and while
we had slowed the flow of blood a natural patch had
formed. Doc gave Reno a tetanus shot and told me to give
him a month's rest and plenty of feed.

Two weeks later the wound had healed, and I believe I
could have put the old horse back into service. But I gave
him a full month to recover, and by July we were back
chasing wild cattle again.

A year after Reno was stabbed by the bull, we were
working a roundup on the McFarland Ranch west of Beaver. The McFarlands had four big pastures that were always hard to gather. The Beaver River flowed through
them on the south end, and this stretch of the river was
badly infested with tamarack brush. You could hardly see
the cattle in the brush, and sometimes when you did see
them you couldn't get them out of it. The tamaracks were
so dense that if you got out in the middle of them, you
could lose your sense of direction.

On the north bank of the river, the country rose
abruptly into some big, rough sandhills, probably the
highest in Beaver County. Not only were they high, but
the closer you got to the river, the heavier and thicker the
brush became in the sinks and valleys between the hills.
This was not the tamarack brush you found along the river,
but skunkbrush, wild plum thickets, and grape vines. They
must have had their roots in water, because they had
achieved a height and density not often found in this dry
country.

That morning we gathered a pasture, penned the cattle

in a set of wooden corrals at the old McFarland homesite, and branded the calves. After we had feasted on Midge McFarland's fried chicken, baked beans, and fresh cherry cobbler, which she brought out in the trunk of her car, we rode upriver to gather another pasture, the biggest and roughest on the McFarland Ranch. We had a crew or eight or ten cowboys, and our plan for the gather was to sweep the river bottom, pop the cattle out of the brush, and push them through two miles of sandhills to a set of pens at the north end of the pasture.

The crew split up and spread out along the bottom. The river was about thirty feet wide and less than a foot deep in most places, and I crossed it and began working the south side with several other cowboys. Once we entered the tamaracks, I lost sight of them and could only hear their whistles and shouts. Half an hour later the cattle we had scared out of the brush came to a path that led to the river. We pushed them down the path and gathered a small bunch on the south bank. I was working with Preacher Hardy and Ron Sallaska on the south side, and Dwain McFarland waited on the north bank to pick the cattle up when we threw them across.

We put them into the river and they waded across, but instead of continuing north, they broke to the west and headed for some heavy tamaracks upriver. Dwain was having trouble holding them and called for help. I was the closest man to him, so I gave Reno the spurs and we hit the river. We almost made it across, but near the north bank he hit some quicksand, buried his right front foot, and nosed into the river. This was the only time I ever saw Reno lose his feet. I flew over his head and landed in the water, still holding the reins in my left hand. When Reno came up, he was carrying his right front foot.

As I led him out of the river, he hopped on three legs and continued to hold the bad foot in the air. Ron and

Preacher had seen the wreck. I told Ron that I couldn't ride the horse out of the bottom and asked his advice.

He thought about it for a minute, and I knew just what he was thinking: This is one hell of a time and place to cripple a horse. "Well, I don't know," he said. "We can't bring a trailer down into this bottom. There's an oil field road about half a mile north of here. If you can lead him to the road, we'll send someone back with a trailer when we get to the pens. It'll be a while, though."

I watched Ron and Preacher disappear into the tamaracks upriver. Their whistles and shouts grew fainter and fainter, until I was alone with my crippled horse, in an eerie silence that hummed with sounds of locusts, deer flies, and mosquitoes.

I soon discovered why Ron had said we couldn't get a pickup and trailer down to the river. The bottom on the north side of the river was covered with willow and cottonwood saplings, tamaracks, salt grass, plum thickets, and grape vines. And the ground was still boggy from early spring rains. Looking into this jungle, most of it as tall as a man's head, I began to wonder if Reno could hobble through it on three legs. Suppose he couldn't? Then what would I do? How in God's name could you get feed and water to a crippled horse in the middle of all this?

I buckled my spurs together and threw them over the saddlehorn, took the reins, and started north. The trip was painfully slow. Reno never once put his injured foot on the ground. Every step seemed to require a huge effort, and I kept expecting him to stop and refuse to move. I would lead him fifty or seventy-five feet, then stop and let him rest a while, start again, hop another seventy-five feet, and rest again.

Reno had the pain of his injury to torment him, but I had the pain of guilt. I had caused the accident by demanding too much of my horse. The Beaver River is a treacherous stream, and firm sand and quicksand often lie side by side, with no markings or shadings to distinguish one from the other. A horse might move very well across the firm sand and then, with no warning, bog down to his knees. I had hot-rodded my horse across the river, and I felt bad about his injury.

Adding to my gloom was the sudden realization that, with Reno out of commission, I would have to finish the roundup season on Gypsy. It struck me as a particularly harsh form of retribution, since I had already concluded that Gypsy's mission in this life was to do me in. As the Good Book said, "A whip for the horse, a bridle for the ass, and a rod for the fool's back." I supposed that Gypsy would be the rod for this fool's back. It was two weeks later that I hung a spur in the back cinch and she tried to drag me to the Big Roundup in the sky.

After what seemed hours, Reno and I finally picked our way out of the river bottom, climbed a steep bank, and came to the oil field road. I pulled off the saddle and bridle and turned him out to graze, knowing that I wouldn't have any trouble catching him. He didn't graze, but stood in the sun with his head down and his leg hoisted. Two hours later one of the cowboys arrived in a pickup, drove me four miles east to the McFarland headquarters, and I got my pickup and trailer and went back for Reno.

Several days later I hauled him to Liberal, Kansas, and had a veterinarian X-ray his leg. Reno had put in years of loyal service on the ranch, and I figured he deserved the best medical treatment available. The vet studied the X-ray and found no broken or cracked bones. Would the horse ever be sound again? The vet shrugged and admitted that he didn't know. At Reno's age, a horse had only an even chance of recovering. He might be crippled for life. As a prescription, the vet suggested "tincture of time": turn him out to pasture and forget about him. In six months, try him out.

So I turned the old fellow out to pasture and tried to forget him. After a few weeks he began walking on the bad leg, slowly and with a limp. By the end of summer the limp had almost disappeared, though you could detect it if you were looking for it. By the middle of October he appeared to be sound, and I decided to give him a test. If he faltered or stumbled, I would probably never ride him again.

I took him out into the west pasture and walked him for half a mile. So far so good. I trotted him for another half mile. Still no sign of weakness. I eased him into a short lope and felt the old familiar surge of power. After spending six months on the sidelines, Reno was ready to fly. But I held him back, aware that his leg might buckle and put us both on the ground. Finally, after we had gone three miles, I turned him loose and let him go. He passed the test.

When I had unsaddled him and turned him out into the horse pasture, I raised my pant legs and found the hair on my calves rolled up in little balls. Yep, old Reno was back on the job.

18
CALIPSO

I had not been on the Crown Ranch very many months before I realized that at some point two or three years down the road, we were going to run out of horseflesh. I thought I should have no fewer than three good saddle horses available at all times, so that I could alternate mounts during roundup season and periods of hard work, and so that I would have extra horses in case one was injured. I had my three work horses in Reno, Gypsy, and Dollarbill, but Reno was getting up in years, Dollarbill lacked the kind of endurance we needed in a horse, and Gypsy was Gypsy.

There were two avenues open to us in building up the work string. We could either buy horses from the outside, or we could raise, break, and train our own colts on the ranch. The first option posed several problems. To buy a good horse, you need cash and enough time to travel around the country looking at horses and swapping until you find the one you want. Since the cattle market had gone to pot in 1974, my employers did not encourage me to

look for ways of spending money or increasing expenses.
Nor did I have the time or inclination to enter the shadowy
realm of the horse trader.

Horse trading is a highly specialized game. To an amateur or part-timer, it can also be slippery. *Caveat emptor* is
the first rule of the game: Let the buyer beware. This is not
to say that all horse traders are dishonest, but that they are
in the business to sell horses. People who deal in horses em-
ploy a multitude of tricks to enhance the appearance of
their animals. This may be something as innocent as having
a line of sales talk or knowing how to show an animal at his
best, or it may mean using cosmetics and tranquilizers. In
ranch country, you can hear many sad tales about the fellow who bought a nice gentle horse on Monday, and on
Tuesday found a bronc in his corral. There is an old saying
that goes "Good horses never sell," and while it is not entirely true, it contains enough wisdom to make you think
twice before you buy a horse on the open market. Unless
you know the horse and trust the seller, you may end up
exchanging your problems for those of someone else—and
his may be worse than yours.

So in August 1974 I decided to breed Momma Mare to
Mark Mayo's Arabian stallion and start building up our
horse herd from the inside. Why an Arabian, when the
quarter horse was preferred by ninety-five percent of the
ranchers and cowboys in the West? I knew Mark's stallion
and had ridden him on several occasions. I knew he was
gentle, smart, and a good hand out in the pasture. Further,
in our kind of ranching operation, with its wild cattle and
sandy country, the Arabian horse's endurance was a good
quality to have. It certainly came out well in Reno. And
finally, there was the matter of convenience. Mark lived
three miles down the road. Momma Mare had built up a
reputation as a hellion and a kicker, and I could deliver her
to Mark's pens without having to load her into a trailer.

In July 1975 she delivered a filly foal that was jet black
except for a white star on her forehead. I called her Calipso.

John, Scottie, and Kris Erickson, 1976.

I don't know why, except that the name seemed to fit. The old mare was a good mother, gave plenty of milk, and raised a good strong foal, but she taught the filly very few civilized manners. In December, when I weaned Calipso and separated her from her mother, she was as wild as a jackrabbit.

"Wild as a jackrabbit" is a common expression in these parts, but in the case of Calipso it was true. Wild animals are motivated by fear. They have no sense of restraint, and, in fact, will respond to restraint by fighting against it. Put a grown jackrabbit into a cage and see what happens. He will kill himself on the wire. He never adjusts to confinement or accepts the fact that he cannot escape.

I found this same unyielding fear in Calipso. When I began working with her, she was nothing but a wild animal. I could see at once that if I crowded her too close, she would maim or destroy herself on the corral fence. But in order to begin training her, I had to put a halter on her head. How would I do that when she was so terrified that she ran from me on sight?

After thinking the problem over, I decided to run her into a loading chute made of wooden timber. It was heavy enough to contain her, tall enough to prevent her jumping out, and free of jagged edges that might cut her if she thrashed around. I eased her in and gave her a minute to adjust and to recognize that she was indeed confined in a pen she could not destroy. Then I leaned over the fence and slipped the halter over her head. She quivered and her eyes grew wide with fear, but she did not thrash. I attached a stout lead rope to the halter, opened the gate, and let her out. I held on to the other end and hoped to break her to lead.

Instead, she broke me to lead. Her natural instinct was to fight the rope, and when I pulled, she pulled. After she had dragged and slung me around the pen for fifteen minutes, I dallied the rope around a stout post, tying it near

the top so that she wouldn't injure her neck when she struggled against it. She fought the rope and wouldn't give up.
When she was so tired that her sides were heaving and her
eyelids drooping, she was still leaning against the rope with
all four feet braced. This wasn't working. I unhooked the
lead rope and ran her back into her pen. There would be
another day.

Several days later—Christmas Eve, in fact—I walked
down to the barn around five o'clock in the evening and decided to spend some time handling Calipso. She was in a
small pen, with the halter on her head, and I wanted to see
if, through kindness and friendly persuasion, I could get
close enough to her head to catch the halter. I had not been
able to do it because she would stick her head in a corner of
the pen, show me her back side, and run as soon as I began
moving toward her head. I got into the pen with her, and
immediately she stuck her head in the corner. I began
stroking her back and hindquarters and talking to her in a
gentle voice.

For some reason she started hopping up and down on
her front legs. This was something new. I had never seen it
before, and I wondered what it meant. At that moment she
let me know. I was standing two feet behind her (that was
stupid and I knew better) when she hopped up on her front
legs, fired her hind feet at me, and landed a direct hit to my
groin.

I hit the ground, moaning and groaning, and crawled
out of the pen on my hands and knees. Though the temperature was near the freezing mark, I had broken out into
a cold sweat. I shucked off my coat and leather vest and
leaned my back against the side of the barn. Half an hour
later I hobbled home, somewhat wiser than before.

It happened that my brother-in-law, Scot Dykema,
was visiting us that Christmas, and two days later we saddled two horses and prepared to halter break the filly. I
chose Reno for the job since he was the calmest horse on the

ranch. We ran Calipso into the loading chute and put a lead rope on the halter. I dallied the rope around the horn and rode off, while Scot rode behind the filly and kept her moving. As expected, she rebellied against the pressure. At first she planted her feet and tried to go backward. I spurred Reno and he leaned into the rope. We sledded Miss Calipso around the horse pasture until she figured out that she wasn't in Reno's league, not where pulling was concerned. Then she started fighting. She raked Reno's back legs with her little hooves and rammed her head into his flanks. He took no notice of her and kept right on going. He didn't even pin his ears back. My impression was that Reno, the old pro, had decided that this pipsqueak of a mare was not worthy of his attention, and he ignored her. After a while Calipso stopped fighting and trotted along beside us. When we returned to the pens half an hour later she was broke to lead.

For the next several months I worked with her on the ground every day. I led her around the pen and gave voice commands. I picked up her feet and brushed her and rubbed under her belly, where she seemed to be particularly goosy. She responded to this training and did not fight me. I continued the ground work for several months. Then I turned her out into the horse pasture. From time to time I got her up and went over the ground training again, just to keep it fresh in her memory. In July 1977, when she turned two years old, I broke her to ride.

I started by climbing on her in the pens and riding her around. After I had done this several times, I was ready to ride her in the pasture. One morning toward the end of August, Mark stopped by and chatted for a while. He had a horse in his trailer and was on his way to ride his river pasture. He asked if I wanted to go along and ride Calipso. I said sure. Mark broke her to load in a trailer in fifteen minutes.

She was nervous when I climbed on her in the pasture,

and she didn't want to move. I took a deep seat and kicked
her with my heels. She came out bucking. I clamped her
and hung on, and after a little flurry she quit. Mark took the
reins and led her to get her started, then handed them back
to me. After a while Calipso was following Mark's horse
and we were off on our maiden voyage. By the time we got
back to the trailer an hour and a half later, she was respond-
ing to commands and even reining a little. She had tried to
buck one more time during the ride, but it had not been
anything serious.

   Once I had gotten her started, I didn't dare stop, lest
she backslide and forget what she had learned. I loaded her
into the trailer and drove over to the middle pasture. This
pasture had a lot of sandy country in it, and that is where I
wanted to ride her. Sandy country is good for green horses.
A horse expends more energy moving through soft sand
than he does on firm ground, and he learns better after
you've put a wet blanket on him—that is, he accepts training better once he has worked off his youthful energy and
has become tired. A second advantage of sand over firm
ground is that a horse cannot buck as hard where the footing is loose. There is also a third advantage—that in the
event the first two points don't work and the horse bucks
you off anyway, sand makes a softer bedding than baked
clay.

   I pointed Calipso toward the sandhills on the east side
of the pasture and started teaching her to neck rein. She did
fairly well the first half hour, though she showed a green
colt's penchant for walking sideways, changing gaits, and
looking at the scenery. Then she got it in her head that she
wanted to go east. I didn't want her to go east and couldn't
allow her to have her way. I pulled the reins and she re-
sisted. I slapped her on the neck and she began hopping and
dancing, threatening to buck if I didn't leave her alone. I
thought this was a bluff and called it. To my surprise, she
dropped her head and began to pitch.

She had pitched with me before and had never managed to throw me, but this time she was operating with a double load of powder. I clamped her and tried to pull up her head. I found her rhythm and stayed with her through three hard jumps. I was still in good shape and thought I had her ridden when, instead of bucking forward, she planted her front legs and sent a shock wave straight up through the seat of my pants. I didn't last long. She put me away with one last jump, and I crashed into a sandhill. It was good soft bedding.

In bucking ability, Calipso compared to my old friend Gypsy as a firecracker compares to a stick of dynamite. She had made a sincere effort, but she lacked the thunder and lightning of a true outlaw. I was riding her bareback when she piled me, and I think that if I had had a saddle under me I could have made it to the whistle. But that sounds a lot like famous last words.

Two months later I rode her at Mark's shipping roundup, which was her debut as a working ranch horse. She was awkward and green, but we finished the day without a major difference of opinion.

The following spring I began riding her at the Beaver Livestock Auction, penning cattle in the yards after they came off the scales. It was excellent experience for her, and she improved every time I rode her. On several occasions we entertained the yard hands with some rodeo, but I got her rode every time.

The most harrowing of these experiences came when, working in an alley twelve feet wide, we were assaulted by a cow on the prod. The cow charged, butted Calipso in the side, and then went under her. For several seconds I was riding Calipso, Calipso was riding the cow, and the cow was trying with all her heart to eat both of us for lunch. The poor mare was terrified. She had thought that cattle ran from horses, and here was one that had turned the tables on her.

We got away from the cow, but she wheeled around and came after us again. This time Calipso didn't wait around to see what would happen. She turned her back on the cow and bucked the length of the alley, with the old cow blowing snot and hot breath on her hocks. When we came to the end of the alley, I bailed off on the fence and left Calipso to take care of herself. She disappointed me. I had hoped that she would give the cow the same dose of hoof medicine that she gave me on Christmas Eve of 1975, and kick her ugly face in. But in cowardly fashion, she bolted and ran to safer quarters. For several months thereafter, every time a cow gave Calipso a stern glance, I had a runaway on my hands.

RANCH FOR SALE

19
SNOW AND BAD NEWS

Keith Good, my boss in Booker, had given me some warning that there were changes in the wind. In late December
he had come up to the ranch and told Kris and me that the
owner was thinking about selling out. As far as Keith
knew, this was still only talk. The sale might occur in three
months, six months, a year, two years, or never. But if the
ranch did go up for sale, I would have to find another job.

The news depressed me and made it hard for me to
function as a ranch manager. Working around cattle and
horses in the heat of summer and the cold of winter, you
must endure hardships and take certain risks. One of the rewards of this kind of life lies in the sense of continuity that
arises from it. You watch a foal from the day it's born. You
watch it grow and develop. You fight it, you train it, you
risk your bones and hide to change it from a wild beast into
a living tool that responds to commands. With cattle, you
check them, feed them, count them, and doctor them when

they're sick. In the spring of the year, you watch the babies hit the ground. You watch them grow and gain weight on summer grass. You round them up in the fall and load them on trucks. And when they go through the sale ring, a fat, sappy, thrifty bunch of steers and heifers, you feel some personal pride, even though they're not your cattle and your name won't appear on the check.

You put something of yourself into animals. It's not that you love them. You just become a part of their rhythms and cycles. Their home is also your home. You see them every day. You suffer together through the heat of August and the northers of January. You work hard and take chances, not because you will make any more money, but because the rhythm and continuity are important. They may not be important to anyone else in the world, but they are important to you.

Through the month of January and half of February I tried to go on about my business, feeding the cattle, chopping ice on the water tanks, and keeping the ranch running. I tried not to think of the future. Then, around the middle of February, I heard that the ranch was on the market and that at least one buyer had been approached. The news would have depressed me under the best of conditions. As it turned out, it came during the worst winter weather we had experienced in four years.

On February 16 this is how things looked to me. My wife and family had gone to Dallas to visit Grandmother Dykema. I had put them on one of the last planes out of Liberal, Kansas, before the airport closed down because of snow. We had eight inches of snow on the ground, and I was having trouble getting around to feed. Thursday morning I looked out the window and saw heavy, wet flakes of snow falling. I was feeding in a half-ton Chevrolet pickup, equipped with a good set of radial mudgrip tires. With a thousand pounds of feed in the back end, I had managed to get around the pastures. But my feed wagon was good only

Erickson chops ice on a frozen windmill tank in January, one of the daily chores on the ranch.

up to about eight inches of snow. At that depth, it began to drag high center and the mudgrips could no longer pull the load. If I fed the cattle today, I would have to put on tire chains.

I put on the chains, loaded up the feed, and started out into the west pasture. The snow was getting heavier and deeper by the minute. I was moving well with the chains, and I figured that as long as I chose my route with care and avoided deep drifts and hidden ruts, I wouldn't get stuck. But then the motor started sputtering. By the time I reached the feed ground in the middle of the pasture, it was missing badly. I called the cows, but very few came in to feed. They had been walking on snow for several days now, and their feet were getting sore. No more than twenty cows came in. I could hear a dozen more bawling in the distance, somewhere behind the veil of snow.

Well, I would try to drive to them if I could get through the snow. I got into the pickup and turned the key. The engine started and died. It did not start again, or even fire. I opened the hood and fiddled with the ignition wires and the carburetor, hoping that luck and fiddling would correct the problem. I suspected the problem lay in the distributor. The pickup was equipped with a new and complicated electronic ignition system, which I think was designed by some fiend in Detroit who wanted to frustrate cowboy-mechanics. I knew nothing about electronic ignitions, and there was nothing I could do about it.

The house was a mile away. The walk would all be uphill and against the north wind. I buttoned up my sheepskin collar and started slogging through the snow. It was snowing hard, and I hoped the wind wouldn't start blowing while I was out in the middle of this pasture.

As I trudged along, I asked myself, "Why am I doing this? The ranch is up for sale and I won't be here in three months. Why should I care whether or not the cattle are fed?" I couldn't think of a good answer.

An hour later I reached the house. My outer garments were soaked with melted snow, and I was sweating from the long walk uphill. I brewed a pot of coffee and pondered my next move. I didn't think there was a chance I could get a mechanic to come out in this kind of weather, but if anyone would, it would be Junior Holleman in Beaver. Junior was a fine mechanic and something of a free spirit. He ran his own shop, worked long hours until he got tired, and then he would lock the doors and go fishing for a week. When he returned, the word would already have spread through town, and he would find cars waiting in his drive.

I called Junior and explained my problem. I expected him to point out that it was snowing outside and to say that he had all the business he could handle in his nice warm shop. But he said he would be right out. I could hardly believe it. An hour and a half later, Junior had my pickup running and I set out again to feed hungry cattle.

In the days that followed, my life became more and more complicated. I lost a tire chain on the pickup, and without chains I had to dig myself out of every snow drift. The temperature fell to ten below zero. A water pipe burst in the ceiling, and as I was eating a peanut butter sandwich for lunch on Saturday, I looked up to see water flowing down the light fixture in the kitchen. The phone went dead. The pickup wouldn't start. The car wouldn't start. The horses walked across the snow-packed cattleguard and left me alone, abandoned, and without transportation.

Sunday night a horrible gale blew in from the north so that Monday morning, when I was supposed to meet my wife and family at the airport, the road out of the ranch was buried under snow drifts four to six feet deep. I had hungry cattle in every pasture. I couldn't get to them. I had pregnant heifers in the little east pasture. I couldn't get to them. The world had become one enormous white wreck, and I was caught in the middle of it. And through all this, I was tormented by the knowledge that, at some point in the near

future, I would be out of a job, out of this strange white
Parthenon in which we had made our home for four years,
and out into the world with two small children and a wife
to support.

It wasn't one of my better weeks.

20
THE LAST ROUNDUP

At last the sun came out and the snow began to melt away
from the countryside. When the roads were cleared for
travel, Keith Good drove up to the ranch and laid out the
plans for the next several months.

The owner had indeed decided to sell the ranch, and
now that the cattle market was on the rise, he wanted to
move quickly. In the middle of April he wanted us to dis-
perse the cow herd. I was to consign the cattle at the Beaver
Livestock Auction, gather a cowboy crew, clear the ranch,
and ship everything to Beaver. I would then sell all the
horses, put the windmills and fences in good shape, and my
job would end May 1, 1979, though Keith said I could stay
until June if I needed more time.

There were moments over the next few weeks when I
felt some bitterness toward the owner for deciding to sell
the ranch. He owned the property and his name appeared
on the abstracts, but in a deeper sense, I had come to think

Bean time. At noon the roundup crew walks up to the Prairie Parthenon for lunch.

of the ranch as mine. I had nursed and cursed it, adopted its rhythm and pace, and applied my ideas and sweat to improve it. In four years I had built up a personal history with the place, and it didn't seem fair that, with the stroke of a pen and the exchange of papers, someone else should have the right to bring that history to an end.

But this has been the lot of the cowboy from the beginning of the cattle business. Though he has become something of a mythical character in American history, he has never owned title to the medium in which the myth was conceived: land. He has owned it with his heart, but that piece of paper in the courthouse vault has never mentioned his name. A cowboy is one who breaks another man's horses, feeds another man's cattle, digs another man's postholes, lives in another man's house, and occupies a piece of earth that belongs to someone else. Sometimes it doesn't seem fair, but that's the way it is.

But I couldn't blame the owner for wanting to sell his ranch, and I could appreciate his reasons for doing it. After forty-five years' association with ranching and cattle, he had concluded that a functioning agricultural unit was a poor place to invest money. On several occasions he had pointed out to me that while his ranch had a paper value of a million dollars or more, his cattle operation had lost money three out of the four years I was there—not because of anything I did or failed to do, but because of the depressed cattle market.

Why, he wondered, should he continue to pay taxes on the land, tie up his capital in a commodity as perishable as cattle, hire someone to manage the property, and lose money at it? Why not take the same amount of money, put it in a bank, and draw interest on it at no risk? Further, he believed that the federal government had committed itself so deeply to urban voters and consumers that it would never again allow farmers and ranchers to make a profit on their operations, and to support this view he pointed to the actions of the last three presidents.

In 1973 Richard Nixon imposed a price freeze on retail beef. In 1975 Gerald Ford shut off exports of American wheat. In 1978 Jimmy Carter increased imports of foreign beef into the United States. All these actions were taken at a time when farmers and ranchers had begun to make a profit, and they all had the same effect: they disrupted orderly marketing trends, sent commodity prices plunging, and left agriculture floundering in an economic climate where profits were suppressed and expenses rose out of control. In each case a president of the United States yielded to pressure from urban and consumer groups and threw agriculture to the wolves.

The owner of the Crown Ranch resented this, and who could blame him? He owned five thousand acres of sand and sagebrush in the Oklahoma Panhandle. Because, during periods of inflation, value moves away from paper currencies and toward commodities of intrinsic value (gold, silver, and land), his ranch had doubled and tripled in value in just a few years, while its productivity had not changed. He had become a paper millionaire whose principal asset, land, was losing money on a regular basis. He finally decided that if he were a millionaire, he might as well cash in his chips, put his money out on interest, and stop worrying about blizzards, broken windmills, and Washington politicians.

I couldn't blame him. If you love ranching and the ranching way of life you'll stay in it until you go completely busted, just because that's the way you're made. But if you don't love it, if you don't enjoy the work, then you ought to cash in, sell out, and move on, because there are easier ways of losing money.

We decided to sell the cattle at Beaver on Wednesday, April 19. The market was still rising and it appeared that we could get a good price. I consigned the cattle with Pack

Hibbs, one of the owners of the auction, and he began calling buyers. Since the process of sorting, shaping, and pairing up the cattle would take some time, he told me to deliver half the herd on Sunday and half on Monday. I lined up trucks for those days and started calling cowboys.

On the morning of Sunday the sixteenth I had a crew of eight. We rounded up the cattle in the west pasture and shipped them off to Beaver. The next morning, which would be the last roundup on the Crown Ranch, I had a veteran crew: Tom Ellzey, Bill Ellzey, Clarence Herrington, Mark Mayo, Virgil Dean, Jim Gregg, and Sandy Hagar. When they arrived at the Prairie Parthenon for coffee, a heavy fog hung over the sandhills and the visibility had dropped to fifty yards. Naturally I caught a lot of flack about the weather, and several of the fellows threatened to quit at the first sign of snow. By the time we hit the saddles and rode out into the middle pasture, the fog had begun to lift. The sun broke through the clouds and left us with a sparkling, clear spring morning.

We gathered the middle and big east pastures without a hitch, which was a nice way to bring things to an end. Who knows? Maybe in four years' time we had taught those crazy cattle some manners.

As we drove the big east bunch toward the pens, a dry norther blew in and sent cowboy hats flying through the air. By the time we began sorting the cattle in the pens, the wind was blowing a gale and our eyes were soon filled with dust and dried manure. But when the truck arrived at ten-thirty, we had our cattle sorted and ready to load.

At noon we went up to the house for lunch. As soon as I walked in the door, the telephone rang. It was Pack Hibbs in Beaver. He said the crew at the livestock auction had been pairing up the cattle we had delivered the day before, and they had come up with a tight-bagged cow. It appeared that we had left her calf in the pasture, and Pack suggested that I turn her out so she could find it. I agreed, and since the cattle truck was coming back after lunch for another load, I told Pack to throw her on the truck.

After lunch we went down to the corrals just as Roy Chockley was backing his truck up to the loading chute. I backed up my stock trailer to another loading chute so that when the cow came off the truck, we could run her down the alley and put her right into the trailer. She was one of those crazy crossbred cows, and she came off the truck in a bad humor. I was standing at the north end of the alley and saw that her head was high and her ears were perked. She beamed the evil eye in my direction, and then here she came. I dived over a gate just in time, and when my feet touched the ground on the other side, I heard the cowboy crew laughing, whistling, and clapping. It wasn't clear whom they were applauding, me or the cow.

We finally got her loaded in the trailer and shut the gate behind her, and I hauled her down to a windmill in the center of the west pasture. When I opened the trailer door, out she came. Now, this old rip had a four-section pasture all to herself, yet when she hit the ground, instead of going off to find her lost calf, she came right back after me. I was minding my own business, trying to latch the trailer gate, when I heard her footsteps behind me. She chased me around the trailer and into the back of the pickup. She stood there, snorting and throwing her head and daring me to step down. Instead, I climbed into the pickup through the window on the passenger side and drove off.

Tomorrow morning I would have to get that lunatic cow and her calf into the corral, load her into the trailer, and haul her back to Beaver. I never should have allowed her off the truck. I knew better.

After we had sent the last truck to town, several of us went up to the house. We passed around a jug of sagebrush thinner and laughed about all the wild times we'd had on the Crown Ranch: the Broken Leg Roundup, the two North Pole Roundups, and all the wrecks and stampedes

we'd ridden through together. We brought out a banjo and
guitar and sang until the shadows grew long. We ended
with a bluegrass version of "Ghost Riders in the Sky," and
after howling the last chorus in four-part harmony, there
was nothing left to squeeze out of the occasion. We had
worked together and ridden together for four years. We
had chased wild cows and had finally loaded them on trucks
and shipped them. The last chorus of "Ghost Riders" was
filled with triumph, cowboy bravado, happiness, and sad-
ness. It had been great working with this crew, but it was
over.

21
THE LAST OUTLAW

My job wasn't quite over, though. I still had that crossbred cow out in the west pasture, and I had to get her to town the next day. I figured it wasn't going to be an easy job, so I asked Bill Ellzey if he could stay the night and help me. He said he would.

It was particularly fitting that Bill and I should go out together after the last outlaw. He had come up to the ranch and helped me settle into the place my first week on the job. He had attended most of the roundups on the ranch, and of course he had participated in that horrid experience in May of 1974, when we had both lost our ropes to wild heifers.

And there was another reason why Bill and I should go out on that last ride. Bill had sold his horse to the Crown Ranch in 1976, and I had recently traded my horse, Dollarbill, to the ranch for Calipso, the little mare I had broke and trained. In one week I would take both Suds and Dollarbill to the Beaver Livestock Auction and sell them through the

ring. This would be Bill's and my last ride on our old
horses.

When we stepped outside that Tuesday morning, we
found the day cold and windy. We saddled Suds and Dollarbill, loaded them into the trailer, and drove out into the
west pasture to find the cow and calf. By sheer luck, we
drove upon the calf in some sandhills on the west end of the
pasture. The calf was bawling and alone, which meant that
the cow had not found him during the night. We roped the
calf, loaded him into the trailer, and drove on east to see if
we could find the cow. We located her on the northeast
end, only a quarter mile from the pens. That was another
piece of good luck, and we told ourselves that this might be
an easy job after all.

Since the cow had shown such a nasty disposition the
day before, I wanted to handle her as gently as possible. Instead of going at her directly with horses and taking the
chance that we might get her stirred up, we would try to
lure her into the pens, using the calf as bait. That wasn't
the cowboy way of doing things, but I had spent the past
four years cowboying wild cattle, and now all I wanted was
to get this hussy off the ranch.

When the calf bawled, the old cow threw up her head
and began to sniff the wind. She must have caught the
scent because she came toward us at a trot. Our plan was
working. I drove slowly toward the pens, and she followed.
We were only fifty yards away from victory when she
stopped and looked at the pens. She didn't go another step.
So we tried another tack. We unloaded the horses, and I
took the calf on the end of my rope and rode toward the
cow. We figured that once she saw her calf, she would stay
with him and we could ease them into the pens. Bill looped
around to the south and got behind her, just in case she
tried to run. I had used this calf-on-the-string trick several
times before and it had always worked.

But not this time. When the cow saw our horses, she

This old man just barely made it through the winter. His feet are broken down, he's in poor condition, and his sunken eyes and shaggy face remind the head cowboy that the bull needs to go to town—yesterday.

threw up her head and went north at a run. Bill opened up
Suds and gave chase. She ran to the northeast corner of the
pasture, spun around several times, and thundered down
the fence to the west. Bill rode hard to get position on her
so that he could turn her into the pens when she came to
them. He got into position and made his move, but the cow
had no intention of turning. Bill had to move in and take
her on in tighter quarters, and when he did, the old rip cut
behind Suds, blew right past, and continued west. Since I
still had a calf on my rope, I couldn't help.

All right, if that's the way she wanted it, we would
have to put a rope on her and drag her into the trailer. I tied
down my calf (we came back later and got him) and went
west to help Bill. I rode and I rode, and still I couldn't see
him or the outlaw cow. At last I found them on the west
side of the pasture, two miles from the point at which the
chase had begun. The cow had covered that distance in ten
minutes' time. I often said that if a man had a string of saddle horses that could run as far and as fast as those Crown-
branded cows, he'd really be a-horseback.

Bill and I stopped to make medicine. Bill said that he
had tried to turn the cow several times but that she had
come after his horse. From then on, he had tried only to
stay up with her. She had stopped running and was standing in a draw near the fence.

I took down my rope. "Well, I guess there's only one
thing left to do."

Bill nodded and gave me an odd smile. I knew that he
was remembering the wreck we had gotten into with those
heifers four years before, and thinking that this crossbred
cow was bigger and nastier than the heifers had been.
Neither one of us wanted to tangle with her, but as long as
she was on the ranch we had to try to gather her up. We
built our loops, split up, and walked our horses forward
into battle.

As we approached, she threw her head into the air,

snorted, and cocked her ears. She took two steps toward
Bill, two steps toward me. She spun in a circle, and then
she plowed through the fence and headed west on the
McFarland Ranch. Bill glanced at me to see if I wanted to
go after her. I grinned and tied up my rope. I'd learned my
lesson four years ago in Mark Mayo's pasture, and I had become an educated man. As far as I was concerned, we had
cleared the ranch.

22
GOOD-BY TO THE HORSES

The cattle sold at Beaver on April 19. Pack Hibbs and his crew did a good job of sorting and shaping them, the market was strong, and they brought top dollar. One draft of young cows with calves brought $530, and several bunches of steers brought sixty-three and sixty-four cents a pound. That was a good price at that time, and everyone felt we had "killed a bear."

For me, the high point of the sale came when the Red Brangus bulls went through the ring. The first bull to sell was the same one that had tried to knock me through a landing mat fence in 1975. When the gate opened, he sprang into the ring like a huge jungle cat. The fellows who were working the ring dived for the fence. The bull charged around, snorting and slinging his head. Then he stopped and started pawing the ground. He threw sand clear across the ring and showered the crowd on the other side. When he had sold, he wouldn't leave the ring and the sale came to a halt. For five minutes he walked around the ring, glowering at the crowd and daring anyone to come over the fence, while the men in the audience pelted him with paper cups, pieces of ice, and cigarette butts. Finally, when he was ready to leave, he swaggered out.

The next bull came through the same way. He would have cleaned the ring, too, but by this time the reputation of the Crown Ranch bulls had already been established, and the men stayed on the fence. While this one was selling, a third bull in a holding pen got one of the yard hands pinned against a wall. Inside the barn, we could hear him yelling for help. Several of the men who were working the yards came running, but there wasn't much they could do. Anyone who went into the pen would get the same treatment. They beat on the bull with whips and canes until he backed away, giving the fellow in the pen enough time to escape. He was as pale as a sheet and had to sit down for a while, but he got out of it with only bruises. It was a good thing the bull didn't have horns.

I must admit that I took wicked pleasure in watching the Crown Ranch bulls raising so much hell. Their performance in the sale ring gave the world a brief glimpse of what I had lived with for four years. Those same bulls had dealt me plenty of misery, and now that I no longer had to work with them, I could sit back and watch them terrorize someone else.

With the cattle out of the way, my next project was to sell the horses. When you sell a horse, you can expect that he will go in one of two directions. If he is young, broke, gentle, and experienced, he will almost certainly go back to work on a ranch somewhere. But if he has some age on him or if he's not well broke, he will be picked up by a cattle trader who will sell him as a packer or killer horse—which means that he will become either pet food or horse meat for the European market.

There is something undignified about a ranch horse

ending his career as pet food, and I wanted to make every attempt to find a home for the horses that had served me on the ranch. As I saw it, Suds was out of danger. He was young and stout, and someone would put him to work. Gypsy might get picked up and used as a brood mare, or she might go to the packers. Dollarbill and Reno were in danger. They were both gentle horses with years of service left in them, but their age would go against them. They were prime candidates for the dog food factory.

I didn't spend much time worrying about Gypsy, after all she had done to me, but for my own benefit I wanted to place her with the Barby Rodeo Company. If she won a spot in the Barbys' bucking string, I would feel a little better about my failure to make a horse out of her—and I could watch someone else take a beating on her.

Around the first of April I mentioned this to Read and Lloyd Barby. They said they would be testing some new horses and bulls at their arena on Sunday afternoon, and if I brought Gypsy down they would try her out. So I loaded her up and hauled her down to Lloyd's place on the Beaver River. They ran her into the chute, and Danny Engleman, a young rodeo cowboy from Beaver, put on his rigging and climbed on. Gypsy began bucking while she was still in the chute, and I figured she would give Danny all the action he wanted.

The gate swung open and out she came. She bucked hard, and every time she jumped, Danny ran his spurs into her shoulders. She bucked out twenty-five feet in front of the chutes and stopped. Danny whipped and spurred but couldn't get her to move. He shrugged, hopped off, and led her back to the chute. Gypsy had just flunked her rodeo test. The old sow.

The week before I took the horses into Beaver to the sale, I talked to several people about Dollarbill and Reno. I hoped that someone in the area would pick them up and give them a good home.

Then, on Wednesday morning, April 26, I walked down to the barn and whistled the horses up to feed for the last time. For the next hour I primped and fussed over Suds, Dollarbill, and Reno. I trimmed their tails, cut the cockleburs out of their manes, trimmed up their feet, washed them, brushed them, and curried them down. I wanted them to look good in the ring. I felt a bit like a mother who was getting her children ready for the first day of school.

I found myself lingering over Reno. I remembered all the flying trips we had made over the ranch, the wild cows we had chased, the time down at Mark's when he had been gored by the bull, the time over on the McFarland Ranch when we had gone down in quicksand. Before I led him to the trailer for the last time, I hugged his neck. He stood perfectly rigid, with his eyes directed straight ahead. If he would miss me, he certainly wasn't going to let me know about it.

I loaded the horses in the trailer and started out for Beaver. As I drove away, I was struck by the emptiness of the horse pasture and the loneliness of that huge white house on the hill, and I knew that when the time came for me to leave the Crown Ranch, I would be ready to go.

At the Beaver Livestock Auction I rode each horse from the trailer to the yards—all but Gypsy, whom I led. Since a horse will sell better if he is ridden through the ring, I had saddled Reno, Dollarbill, and Suds. I had no intention of riding Gypsy through the ring. She would bring more money if I did, but she also might throw me into the nickle bleachers. Gypsy had had her chances to do me in, and she wasn't going to get another.

Several buyers had gathered outside the sale barn, and they studied each horse as I rode him to the yards. Among them were Jim Gregg and his father. They had come to bid on Reno. I was glad to see them. If they bought the horse, he would have a good home.

John, Scottie, and Kris in the west pasture, looking south toward
the Beaver River.

The Crown Ranch horses were scheduled to sell right after the baby calf sale, and when the calves started coming through, I went back to the sorting pens where the horses had been brought up. I didn't even lead Gypsy through the ring. I just removed the halter and let her go. I told the auctioneer the truth: she had been used as a ranch horse, I had roped off her, and she had raised a foal. She brought $320 and probably ended up a brood mare, a fate which was too good for her.

Next came Dollarbill. When I climbed in the saddle, I could sense that he was nervous and I was afraid he might try to buck in the ring. He often kicked up when you first got on him and touched him with a spur. "You old fool," I said as the gate opened in front of us, "if you pile me in front of all these people, I'll get up and cut your throat." He kicked up a little bit, but it didn't amount to much. I rode him back and forth in the ring, then jumped off, pulled the saddle and bridle, and threw them on the rail around the sale ring. I heard only the final bid as I went back to get another horse. Dollarbill brought $390. I didn't hear who had bought him, and I didn't want to know. Even after the sale I didn't ask, but I feel sure that he went to the packers.

I rode Suds in next, and the bidding got hot. Suds was a good-looking horse, the kind the local buyers liked. As I rode him around the ring, I looked up and saw a familiar bearded face out in the crowd. He smiled and nodded his head in a greeting. I waved back. It was Bill Ellzey, who had driven up from the LZ Ranch to watch his old horse sell.

While the bidding was still going on, I bailed off and pulled the saddle. When the saddle came off, the bidding stopped and Suds sold for $465. I was surprised that he didn't bring more money, and later, when I mentioned this to Jake Parker, a local horse breaker and cowboy, he said that when I pulled the saddle, the buyers saw that Suds was a little sway-backed, and that had killed the bidding.

When Suds left the ring, I came back in on Reno. I tried to put on a show with him, to demonstrate his quickness. When someone in the crowd yelled, "What's his age?" the auctioneer stopped the bidding and asked me how old a horse he was. On impulse, I fudged. I said he was "about fifteen." The bidding started up again, but it wasn't hot. Reno sold for $360.

After we had auctioned off the saddles and tack, I stepped outside for a breath of air and found Jim Gregg. Jim and I were good friends, and he knew how I felt about Reno.

"We bid on him but Dad didn't want to pay that much for an old horse."

I understood. The high demand for horsemeat in Europe had made packer horses more attractive to buyers, and the packer buyers were paying more for marginal horses than farmers and ranchers could afford to pay. In buying a horse, the packers had one clear advantage over the country folks: they didn't have to worry about pasture and feed bills, or whether the horse was sound.

I asked who bought Reno. Jim mentioned one of the cattle buyers who attended the sale every week and bought in larger numbers. "I went up and asked him what he was going to do with the horse," Jim continued. "He said, 'Send him to the killers. He'll bring forty cents a pound hanging on the rail.' "

I nodded. In the back of my mind I saw Reno hanging in a huge cooling room, headless and stripped of his skin. Horsemeat for the French.

Isn't it strange that the fate of a cow horse in the Oklahoma Panhandle could be determined by the appetites of people living half a world away? But that's what happened, and it didn't make a happy ending to my four years on the Crown Ranch.

23
EPILOGUE

I have given you a leading character in Mr. Reno Horse. I have described him as gallant and noble and worthy of your admiration. I have told you that on April 26, 1978, he sold through the ring at the Beaver Livestock Auction, that he sold to a packer buyer, and that he was destined to hang on the rail in a cooling room and eventually find his way to Europe, where he would be served up in a Paris cafe under the French name for cow horse steak.

That's a lousy way to end a book. Personally, I prefer a happy ending to one that is grim and depressing. But it would be dishonest to manipulate the facts just to improve the story, and I have reported the facts—except for a few details about the fate of Reno.

The day after I sold the horses at the auction, I learned that the packer buyer who had bought Reno had, for reasons unknown, decided that he didn't want him. So instead of hauling him away, he had dumped him off on Ned Kygar, the manager of the auction. Ned traded in horses and cattle, but at that time he was out of the horse-trading business. He didn't want Reno either, but to please one of his good customers, he had taken him. Reno was still in Beaver and would probably be there until Ned could haul him to a horse sale.

Two days later I was walking down the street in Perryton, Texas, my old home town. A pickup pulled over to the curb and a man stepped out. It was Don Beck, the head football coach at Perryton High School, who had been my football and track coach when I was a quasi-athlete at PHS. Coach Beck told me that he was retiring from coaching and moving to Montana to run a small ranch.

"I heard you had some horses for sale," he said, "and I wanted to ask you about them. I'm looking for some gentle horses to take up to Montana."

I stared at him for a moment. Was this an angel sent to rescue old Reno from the hungry French?

I told him about Reno and he was interested. Reno sounded like just the kind of horse he had been looking for. Two days later he and Ned got together, agreed on a price, and Coach Beck bought himself a horse. Reno was saved.

As I write this today, I am located on another ranch in Beaver County, and Reno has gone to Montana. I can see him now, standing in a green meadow with the Montana mountains blue in the distance. I'll never see him again, but I'll never forget him.

So there you are. I have given you a happy ending, and the best part of it is that it actually happened this way.